NEAR

VISION

of

ARMAGEDDON

V I S I

ARMAG

THE COUNT DOWN BEGINS

401 **40** **53:57**

HRS   MIN.   SEC   MSEC

A MICHAEL BAY FILM

ONS

f

EDDON

HYPERION >> NEW YORK

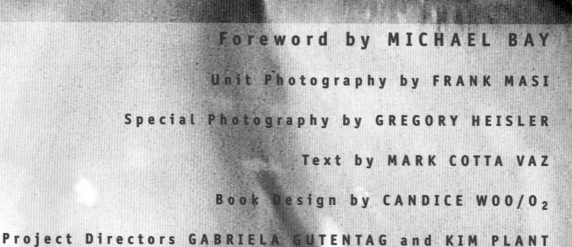

Foreword by **MICHAEL BAY**

Unit Photography by **FRANK MASI**

Special Photography by **GREGORY HEISLER**

Text by **MARK COTTA VAZ**

Book Design by **CANDICE WOO/O₂**

Project Directors **GABRIELA GUTENTAG** and **KIM PLANT**

Text copyright© 1998 Disney Enterprises, Inc.
Photographs copyright© Touchstone Pictures and Jerry Bruckheimer, Inc.
www.ARMAGEDDON.com
Soundtrack available on Columbia CDs and cassettes.

A Roundtable Press Book

Printed in the United Kingdom by Butler & Tanner Ltd, Frome & London

For Roundtable Press
Directors: Susan E. Meyer, Marsha Melnick, Julie Merberg
Computer Production: Steven Rosen
Editor: James Waller
Manufacturing Consultant: Bill Rose

For Hyperion
Jennifer Lang

Design Associate: Rosana Rivera

ISBN 0-7868-8347-2
First Edition
10 9 8 7 6 5 4 3 2 1

All photographs by Frank Masi, except as indicated:

Gregory Heisler
pages 3 (inset), 6 (inset), 13, 14-15, 19, 20-21, 36-37, 43, 44 (top inset), 98, 100 (top
inset), 101 (bottom inset), 108 (top inset), 108-109, 120 (inset), 120-121, 133 (top
inset), 133 (bottom inset), 134-135, 138 (inset), 139 (inset), 142-143, 144 (left), 145,
147, 148-149, 155, 156, 157 (left inset), 159 (top inset), 159 (center inset), 159 (bottom inset), 168 (top inset), 168 (bottom inset)

Tom Vollick
page 71 (inset)

Tracy Bennett
page 95 (inset)

Tory Von Wolfe
page 152

CONTENTS

FOREWORD

In 1977 I made my first "space movie." Using some string model spaceships, mom's Super 8 camera and some illegal fire-crackers, I proceeded to make a movie about an enemy spaceship attacking my train set's quaint little town. I was only thirteen, but I thought the three-minute movie was quite good. My parents, however, didn't. Somehow the explosions got out of control, and the fire department rushed to the rescue to put out the fire in my bedroom. I was grounded.

Flash forward nearly twenty years—I was introduced to the concept that would become my second space movie. In October 1996, on a Tuesday afternoon, I got a call from Jonathan Hensleigh, a writer I had worked with on the *The Rock*. He said, "Michael, you know all those loathsome asteroid movies? Well, what about making a great asteroid movie?"

Jonathan's story unfolded in three sentences: A global killer is traveling on a collision course with Earth, and NASA must enlist the help of the world's best deep-core driller and his team to fly up to and land on the asteroid. They must drill into the asteroid's fault lines, plant a nuclear device, and trigger it. The only problem: Everything goes wrong.

In this premise lay a staggering number of tantalizing possibilities. The core of the story was an epic tale, but more important, it provided a canvas broad enough to create characters that were heroic and yet intrinsically American, and very human.

The idea that something so devastating could happen to Earth, that mankind could be faced with total annihilation, with no recourse, no place to hide, grabbed my attention. And then to place the fate of the world in the hands of the space program and a small, ragtag team of quintessential underdogs—thrust into the role of the world's warriors—was a huge movie idea.

Jonathan and I distilled the best of our collective ideas, then powered through the story in three quick weeks. When we went in to pitch the story to Joe Roth, Chairman of the Walt Disney Studios, we had no idea how he would respond. We were, after all, presenting an awesome undertaking that would require an astounding level of resources. We were asking Disney to take on a potential blockbuster, but an enormously ambitious film, conceptually and monetarily.

After twenty minutes he said, "Wow—this is going to be Disney's biggest movie of '98. Let's call it *Armageddon*." Even then we knew it would be the studio's largest movie ever. After the meeting, we were basically given a green light to make the movie. I turned to Jonathan and said, "You know, we just pitched an epic film. What did I get myself into?"

From the start, I wanted to present the space program with the luster of its Right Stuff days, the race to the moon, when NASA rocket launches led the evening news instead of receiving barely a mention, and before the historic *Challenger* tragedy took its toll on the program and diminished the collective awe of a nation. I wanted to portray it with the innocence of a bygone era, as I remembered it from the first grade, where I once laboriously scratched out a crayon drawing of Alan Shepard golfing on the Moon. Astronauts were my heroes back then, as I think they were for everyone. Beyond that, I wanted to create a film that would resonate with anyone who has dreamed of accomplishing the impossible. For anyone who believes that nobility, valor, courage, and sacrifice are not just pretty words, and are not things of the past. Against this backdrop, I wanted to add a love story, to create a broader, richer human context.

To do this we needed bigger-than-life characters who also had little intimate moments that made them real, against an arsenal of technically astounding special effects. We found those characters in the form of Harry Stamper and his crew. Played by Bruce Willis, Stamper is a Texas oil driller recruited by NASA to land on the asteroid. Stamper is Everyman forced to face the unfaceable. He must rise above his fears, shore up his emotional underpinnings, and confront the abyss of mankind's worst nightmare. He is a simple man, who through his actions becomes a hero far beyond his own imaginings. His final act is defining, life-affirming, and, ultimately, redemptive.

With the complexity of the characterizations, we knew we would need an intelligent, provocative, and humorous script, which we got from additional writing by J. J. Abrams, Tony Gilroy, Scott Rosenberg, Shane Solerno, and Ann Biderman. We would also need to assemble a vast battery of talent, both in front and behind the camera. I found myself continually inspired by the energy and resourcefulness of the 1,700 people who worked on the film, by the astounding technical effort, but especially—first, last, and foremost—by Jerry Bruckheimer, who, at the development stage pushed the film to the next level, and to whom I owe a huge debt of gratitude. Jerry had tapped me to do two earlier films for him: *Bad Boys* and *The Rock*. He has produced a juggernaut of box-office hits, some of the biggest films of all time. He is a consummate filmmaker, a director's producer, and without him, this would have been a very different film.

From the beginning, we knew that the making of this film hinged on the cooperation of the Air Force and everything NASA had to offer. My executive producer, Jim Van Wyck went on a tireless quest to get this cooperation. It

6

ABOVE:

*First assistant director
K. C. Hodenfield.*

RIGHT:

*Director/producer Michael Bay and producer
Jerry Bruckheimer.*

started at Cape Canaveral. Jimmy told the story of *Armageddon* to Bill Johnson, Kennedy Space Center's Deputy Chief of Media Services, while standing on the launchpad next to a space shuttle. When Jimmy ended the story twenty minutes later, Bill Johnson had tears streaming down his cheeks. It was the heroic, noble story that ultimately convinced everyone to lend support for the film.

As you will read in the pages to follow, the Air Force and NASA's combined participation was nothing short of extraordinary. They provided access to shoot actual space shuttles and the most exotic Air Force aircraft in the American arsenal. They allowed us to photograph an estimated $20-billion in hardware—a far cry from the string and model space ships I was used to.

Their cooperation included allowing us to shoot on the sky-high launchpad and walkway leading to a space shuttle being readied for launch. Even to cast and crew members who have shot in the unlikeliest of places, the experience of shooting this historic walkway was unforgettable. Each of us struggled to reconcile the reality of standing amidst this towering hardware representing so much human effort with our own lingering images of space shots from childhood. It was truly humbling, inspiring, and a forceful reminder that the men and women of NASA are the flesh-and-blood personification of the heroism and the spirit of cooperation we were portraying on screen.

As I write this, I'm putting the final touches on *Armageddon*. Ironically, *The New York Times* sits on my desk with the headline: ASTEROID IS EXPECTED TO MAKE A PASS CLOSE TO EARTH IN 2028. When I first saw the article, it seemed that life was imitating art. But the truth is, our material was fashioned from a very real threat. And although some might surmise from our film that NASA is capable of undertaking a mission like ours in *Armageddon*, NASA cautions that this type of defense will not be possible for another twenty to thirty years. Maybe longer.

And as this project draws to a close, I think I have a better idea why this material drew me in so completely. I made this movie for many reasons and for many people, but in the end, I made it for the six-year-old kid who long ago penned a drawing of Alan Shepard, and for other kids like him. I made it for anyone who dreamed of space and for those who believe that space exploration remains a powerful symbol of the best that our country, our institutions, and our people, have to offer.

For Jerry, myself, and my wonderful crew and cast, we have put our hearts into this film—we welcome you to our world of *Armageddon*.

Michael Bay

8

The Mir-like Russian Space Station: refueling stop for the shuttles of mission Armageddon. Illustration by Wil Rees.

THE DREAM FACTORY

When Walt Disney's *Fantasia* premiered on November 13, 1940, at New York City's Broadway Theater (the very house in which Mickey Mouse had debuted in *Steamboat Willie* some 12 years earlier), one of the animated feature's ambitious vignettes opened with a flight through outer space. In this sequence, we see our home galaxy, as if from light-years away, swimming in a dark infinity. As we move in closer, the Earth appears, boiling in the volcanic throes of creation. The molten seas cool, life begins and eventually crawls onto the land, where it evolves into the dinosaurs. To the strains of Igor Stravinsky's *Rite of Spring*, the Earth's birth cycle ends as the Sun mysteriously heats up, the planet warms, the seas dry up, the land is scorched by the heat, and the dinosaurs march off into extinction.

9

That *Fantasia* year also marked a milestone in the evolution of the Walt Disney Company, as Walt moved his studio from the one-story white stucco and two-story Spanish Revival–style buildings it had occupied on Hollywood's Hyperion Avenue to a state-of-the-art facility on a 50-plus-acre tract in nearby Burbank.

More than half a century later Walt Disney Studios continues to flourish on that Burbank lot. In the 1990s, the studio's venerable old buildings have been joined by fantastic new structures, including an animation facility whose entryway tower is shaped like the magical wizard's hat Mickey wore in the *Sorcerer's Apprentice* sequence of *Fantasia*.

In 1997 the Burbank facility was the epicenter of the production of one of the most ambitious live-action features in the company's history: *Armageddon*, a 1998 Touchstone Pictures release whose story embraces science facts more terrifying than any science fiction. As with *Fantasia* so many decades ago, movie houses around the world would once again play out, in flashes of projected light, images of the Earth vulnerable in space. Once again, life on the primordial planet would be destroyed by a disaster—in the opening credits, no less. But this Disney production would be in tune with contemporary scientific consensus that the dinosaurs died in the aftermath of an asteroid's collision with Earth some 65 million years ago.

"Global killers"—that's what scientists call these asteroids that, though they need be no more than a few miles across, can in the instant of impact release a burst of energy massive enough to spell The End of Everything. *Armageddon* would in fact be released only a few years after just such an asteroid had bypassed Earth by a margin closer than the distance to the Moon—a near-miss by cosmic standards.

The film, brought to life by Jerry Bruckheimer Films and directed by Michael Bay (with Gale Anne Hurd's Valhalla Motion Pictures also producing), would adhere throughout to what Hurd calls "verisimilitude." In consultations with astronauts and asteroid experts, the production team shaped the film's dramatic premise, basing their terrifying tale not only on accurate calculations of a potential asteroid impact but also on a theoretically possible response human beings might make to defend their planet—landing a manned ship on the rock, drilling a hole into it, planting an atomic bomb, and then detonating the explosive by remote control. So might a collision-course asteroid be blown off course and doomsday averted.

11

Top deck of the Russian Space Station. Illustration by Tani Kunitake.

The twist in *Armageddon* is that it isn't career astronauts who are called on to save the world. Instead, the off-planet drill-and-bomb team is led by the world's greatest deep-earth oil driller, a character named Harry Stamper (played by Bruce Willis), and his two-fisted crew of very earthbound roughnecks.

As befits the ambitions of producer Bruckheimer (who with his late partner, Don Simpson, produced such worldwide box-office sensations as *Flashdance, Beverly Hills Cop I* and *II,* and *Top Gun*) and director Bay (whose first two features were the Simpson/Bruckheimer-produced action films *Bad Boys* and *The Rock*), Armageddon goes for the "real deal" flourishes that make movie-making an adventure, from location work at an oil rig in the Gulf of Mexico to negotiations with the U.S. Air Force—convincing the military to park billion-dollar bombers within camera range.

But it would be the doors opened by the National Aeronautics and Space Administration (NASA) that would provide *Armageddon*'s makers with truly unprecedented footage—from actors in real spacesuits diving into a high-security pool used to train bona fide astronauts to an actual space-shuttle launch, which, in moviemaking's surreal blend of fact and imagination, is transformed into the launch of *Armageddon*'s doomsday squadron.

As soon as *Armageddon* was given the green light by Joe Roth, Chairman of Walt Disney Studios, the production began pulling a stellar cast and crew into its orbit. On Disney's Burbank lot, several soundstages would undergo a metamorphosis that occurs when movie magic is being conjured—especially Soundstage 2 (located just off Mickey Avenue), where the film's rugged live-action asteroid set would be created.

Along with the commitment to superlative production values would come the pressures weighing on a picture tagged with blockbuster status. "On a big movie you're spending a ton of money every day, and the meter starts ticking from the minute you get up in the morning," says producer Jerry Bruckheimer. "You've got a studio that's relying on you to bring the movie in on budget. That's the key to all this—it's called show business. And my responsibility is to make sure we're giving the audience something they'll want to pay to see more than once."

Flash forward to Disney's Burbank lot, the third week of January 1998. The studio's abuzz with all the energy of a Hollywood dream factory at full throttle, the production moving at top speed from early morning to late at night. "We were supposed to have wrapped and we're still shooting," shrugs Armageddon production designer Michael White as he stands on the high ground of the craggy asteroid set. In a pitlike depression below, a circle of lights and cameras is trained on two of the spacesuited roughnecks being showered with rocky debris. "When I jumped aboard a year ago they were already furiously writing and conceiving. I'm still designing, and I have to find a couple more locations. It's not like we first build everything for the movie and it's all ready to go. It's an ongoing process. That's just the way it is with these big pictures."

These are the last days of *Armageddon*, and the cast and crew, like exhausted marathon runners with the finish line in sight, are "picking up everything we can," as one actor puts it: from major action scenes shot on the asteroid set to connecting pieces filmed on insert stages. From soundstage to soundstage, bright movie lights are rigged from floor to rafters and cables lie as thick as jungle vines across the floor. The shooting stages grow misty with the steam and smoke used to enhance atmosphere and help make live-action "read" on film. There's a constant flow of foot traffic: producers and stars walking alongside grips and lighting technicians; department heads talking business on their cell phones or huddling in groups to plot out the next challenge.

12

ABOVE: *Spacesuited hero wields the clapper as cameras begin to roll.*

RIGHT: *Bruce Willis [Harry Stamper].*

FOLLOWING PAGES: *On the asteroid set, director Michael Bay [left, center] and director of photography John Schwartzman [right] watch a take from behind the video monitors. Script supervisor Karen Golden is at far left, and key grip Les Tomita kneels at right.*

ABOVE: *The roughnecks and astronauts on their final march to the shuttles.*

An oasis for production principals and *Armageddon* performers is the trailer area a stone's throw from the soundstages. This parking-lot haven is where Bruce Willis goes to relax after a hard day of saving the world. Between takes, other cast members relax in their own trailers, among them Liv Tyler (who plays Harry Stamper's daughter, Grace) and Ben Affleck (A. J. Frost, Harry's pain-in-the-neck protégé who's in love with Grace—much to the senior Stamper's dismay). This all-star trailer court is also the place where producer Bruckheimer can conduct business or director Bay can take a break from filming.

Lunch hour arrives, and Bay is in his trailer, getting some welcome R&R from shooting in the depths of the asteroid set. "It's been a rough week," he sighs, stretching. The 33-year-old director usually has energy to burn, but the rigors of making dreams come true have to take their toll: while most first-unit stages of production wrap within 60 days, *Armageddon* is at the 100-day mark, with several more weeks ahead, including a location shoot at an oil rig in the Gulf of Mexico. Things have gone smoothly—"The studio's been great," Bay reports—but the complex production, with its unprecedented location shoots, soundstage work, and visual effects, has been pushing the envelope for even the most ambitious Hollywood blockbuster. Bay admits the crew is "a little beaten down, real tired." By his estimate some 1,700 people will have worked on the production by the time *Armageddon* wraps.

Today, Bay is thinking back on the months of filming he's already done, of the sheer scale of the hardware he saw while shooting behind the scenes at NASA: "The NASA people themselves call their place 'the land of the world's biggest toys,'" he says. Then Bay shakes his head as he describes getting up close to the Air Force's top-secret B-2 Stealth wing bomber.

"The B-2 is a two-billion-dollar aircraft," he marvels. "It's so bizarre: You look inside and it's just this killing machine. The canopy is very strange. The skin isn't made of metal but of some kind of composite material. The bomb-bay doors are as thin as a knife blade and they match up perfectly, with no gap at all. They have armed soldiers standing around the bomber because you're not allowed to see the back—there's this top secret design where the exhaust comes out."

This is the late-January week when the unveiling of *Armageddon* will begin, during the second quarter of the Super Bowl. In that high-priced commercial spot, the film's fictional NASA hero, Dan Truman (played by Billy Bob Thornton), will be seen gravely informing the president that the mysterious explosions that have hit New York City and elsewhere are the result of basketball-sized meteorites, merely the heralds of a global-killer asteroid on a collision course with Earth. The production team is abuzz with the excitement this spot will create, and the mere thought is a morale booster.

THE PRODUCER

Jerry Bruckheimer's success in Hollywood borders on the unbelievable. His films have generated billions, and their influence extends far beyond the popcorn-munching set: the Navy used Top Gun, the jet-jockey saga that thrust actor Tom Cruise into the rarefied heights of movie superstardom, as a recruitment vehicle. Bruckheimer's films are the kind of productions that provoke learned discussions about "defining a decade."

"Audiences have this notion that producers are the money men," says Bruckheimer. "I'm not. I'm a filmmaker. My choices for projects are all driven by talent and material. Michael Bay's talent and the material itself is what gravitated me to *Armageddon*. Actually, Michael kind of dragged me into this extravaganza.

"I have to get behind an idea before I conjure up the energy to climb the mountain. Every time you finish and release a picture you're starting out at the bottom of the mountain again. The more success you've had, you look up and the mountains just keep getting bigger and bigger. The logistics don't scare me, but it's a daunting task.

"As a producer, what you do is slowly put the team together, trying to get the best in their field. You're constantly talking to talent to get them involved in your train ride—and hopefully it's not a train wreck. You start with your core team of filmmakers: the director, production designer, your cinematographer and film editors. Of course, casting is key.

"We're accused of being loud and having a lot of explosions, but to me those are just punctuations, they're certainly not what it's all about. Character-driven action pieces are what I love. My favorite movies are the kind David Lean made, and when you look at *Bridge on the River Kwai* and *Lawrence of Arabia*, they're big action, big scope, and big epic—but they're all character driven."

If you clear away the smoke from all those gunfights, car crashes, and explosions, Bruckheimer contends, you'll see all the story and heart he puts into his movies. He still has dreams—notably a desire to make the kind of old-fashioned epics that marked the career of director David Lean.

"For *Armageddon*, Michael carried the weight on his shoulders like a real field commander. It was a humongous undertaking for a young director. He had a lot of responsibility directing *The Rock*, but this is a story that goes way beyond earthly things. We're in outer space and on an asteroid. There's an enormous amount of effects, more than I've ever done before. The effects budget alone on this movie was more than *Bad Boys* cost.

"What I like about making movies is you become part of a lifestyle you'll never in your life experience again, or that an audience will never experience. On *Top Gun* I got to be a jet fighter pilot with Tom Cruise, training with the Top Guns. On *Armageddon* I got to hang with the NASA astronauts and scientists, to look at all their toys and watch our actors play with them. It's fun to be dropped into someone else's world and live their life for a moment in time.

"Audiences are now demanding enormous amounts of entertainment, so you've got to give them something exciting, funny, romantic. I always say we're in the transportation business because we transport you from one reality to another.

"That's our game—to really give audiences a thrill ride. If I can take you for two hours and make you forget everything that's going on in your life and just get you absorbed in our story, our characters, our world, then I've done my job."

ABOVE: *Bruckheimer shares a laugh with Liv Tyler, who plays Grace Stamper, the daughter of hero Harry.*

RIGHT: *Producer Jerry Bruckheimer.*

340   37   40:20
HRS   MIN   SEC   MSEC

PART ONE

DOOMSDAY SCENARIO

They called the kings together at the place called, in Hebrew, Armageddon. The seventh angel emptied his bowl into the air, and a voice shouted from the sanctuary, "The end has come." Then there were flashes of lightning and peals of thunder and the most violent earthquake that anyone has ever seen since there have been men on the earth. The Great City was split into three parts and the cities of the world collapsed. . . . Every island vanished and the mountains disappeared. . . .

    —Revelation 16:16–21 (*Jerusalem Bible*)

At 4:49 a.m. Eastern Standard Time, the shuttle *Atlantis* disappears in space. Hours later, without warning, a meteor shower pummels the Eastern Seaboard . . . . The damage is only a precursor: an asteroid the size of Texas is headed our way at 22,000 mph. Its impact would mean the end of mankind. With only 18 days to spare, NASA discovers the "Global Killer" bearing down on Earth.

    —Touchstone Pictures, *Armageddon* publicity release

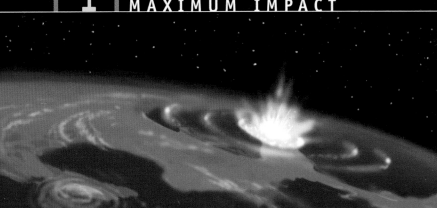

It was during the Christmas season of 1968 that human beings for the first time rocketed free of Earth's gravity en route to the first manned orbit of the Moon. That *Apollo 8* crew— James Lovell, Frank Borman, and William Anders—were the first earthlings to see the planet whole from the loneliness of space, the first to appreciate from afar the home world of blue waters and white clouds: the "grand oasis," as Lovell would describe it.

Author Lewis Thomas, in his classic work *The Lives of a Cell*, similarly describes a Mother Earth that lives and breathes for all the life upon it. Its atmospheric membrane even shelters terrestrial life from deadly meteors, turning space-traversing rocks into falling stars to make a wish upon. "Without this shelter, our surface would long since have become the pounded powder of the moon," Thomas concludes. "Even though our receptors are not sensitive enough to hear it, there is comfort in knowing that the sound is there overhead, like the random noise of rain on the roof at night."

But even that protective atmosphere wouldn't protect the world from a big-enough asteroid. The end-time visions of Revelation, in which the forces of good and evil gather at Armageddon for the final battle of human history, tell of fire and stars crashing down from the heavens. It's virtually an account of a doomsday asteroid hit.

At a January 1998 meeting of the American Astronomical Society, the Los Alamos National Laboratory presented its computer-simulation projections of an asteroid hit. The report read like the passage from Revelation. A story in the January 8, 1998, edition of *The New York Times* noted that the researchers' conclusions "sound like the storyline for Hollywood's next disaster movie." But the creators of *Armageddon* didn't have to embellish the premise—the terrifying science would suffice all by itself.

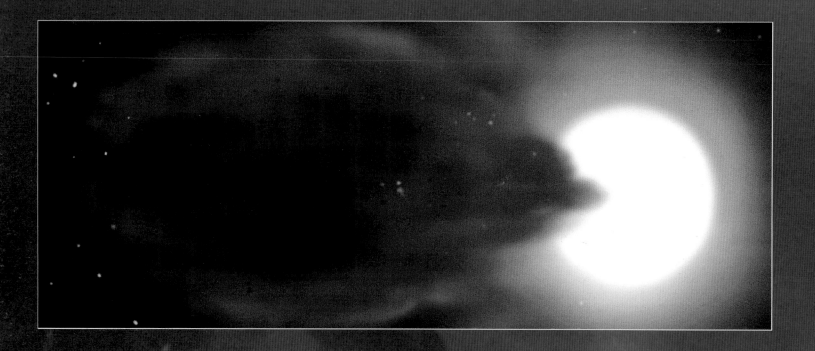

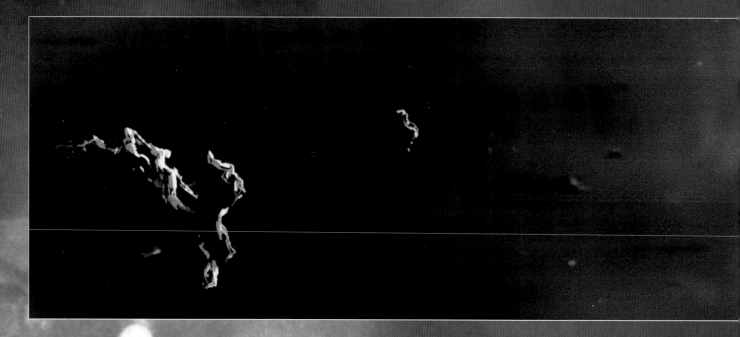

Dream Quest Images concept art of the ancient asteroid hit that destroyed the dinosaurs. According to technical consultant Ivan Bekey, an asteroid of that size, which was probably five or six miles across, is thought to hit Earth once every ten million years. The film imagines an asteroid "the size of Texas."

"I think we would have found out by now if something that big was in Earth's orbit," Bekey says, "but if a comet from way out in the solar system hit one of these large asteroids it could change its orbit enough to send it into an Earth-crossing orbit." Concept art by Mike Meaker.

INSETS:

Concept art for overall look of asteroid, showing shock waves, erupting gas and debris and turbulence at tail. Dream Quest Images computer-generated art by Mike Meaker.

BACKGROUND: Roughneck driller on the asteroid [shot in South Dakota].

"What we wanted on this film was complete verisimilitude—you are there!" explains producer Gale Anne Hurd, whose films include such seminal visions of the fantastic as the *Terminator* movies, *Aliens*, and *The Abyss*. "We tried to keep a lot of this film in the realm of the possible. And when you start doing research and realize that we've mapped so little of the sky, that's kind of frightening. Because an asteroid hit could easily wipe us out."

It was through NASA that the production was put in touch with Ivan Bekey, recently retired after nearly 18 years as one of the space agency's think-tank wizards and a man whose own company, Bekey Designs, Inc., continues to ask big questions about the future. Bekey's scientific know-how would provide *Armageddon* with the "what if?" calculations for a Texas-sized asteroid impact.

"There's a threshold somewhere between half a mile and six miles in diameter in which you begin to have devastating effects," Bekey explains. "What happens when an asteroid hits is the sky turns black from all the debris thrown up into the atmosphere, no sunlight reaches the Earth, all plants and many species die. But eventually life regenerates. This movie postulates an asteroid 600 miles across, a hundred times the size of the one that killed off the dinosaurs. Such a rock could extinguish all possibilities of life regenerating.

"Let me tell you what would happen if a Texas-sized asteroid hit. First, it would be so massive it would come through the atmosphere without really being slowed down. When it hit, all of its momentum would transform into energy in a fraction of a second—that's a *trillion* 10-megaton atomic bombs being blown off at once. All the dirt and debris thrown up into the atmosphere would cause total darkness, and all plant life would die. My rough calculations show the shock waves from the impact would flatten an area at least the size of the United States, and worldwide there'd be earthquakes a hundred times more powerful than the quake that leveled San Francisco in 1906. Even if the asteroid didn't hit directly in the ocean there would be tsunamis, these half-mile-tall waves that would inundate the entire world, drowning coastal areas and flooding hundreds of miles inland. All surface life would die. Even if some life continued to exist—such as a few primitive life forms in the deepest oceans—it would take millions of years to evolve again. It would be a total disaster!"

Part of *Armageddon*'s storytelling strategy is to foreshadow the devastation of maximum impact. A little taste of the doomsday that's in the offing is conjured up by "advance" meteorites that hit Manhattan, blowing cars and buses to smithereens and even slicing off the spire of the Chrysler Building.

The impacts of these meteorites—though mere cosmic motes—instantly grip the imagination: if you think these blasts are bad, imagine what'll happen when something the size of a

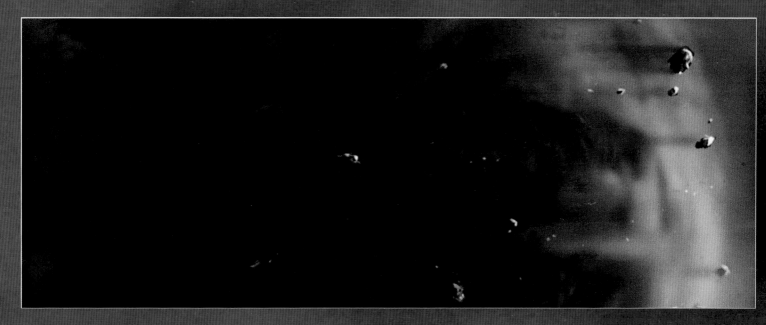

26

Dream Quest Images final concept art for the Armadillo jump
on the other side of Three Spires Ridge, by Mike Meaker.

small moon crashes into the planet at 22,000 miles per hour! Making it all look real would require complex location shoots in New York City and Los Angeles, live-action pyrotechnic effects and stunts, work with scale models, and digital visual effects—basically the entire playbook of movie magic.

Helping craft the design of the meteorite-impact sequence was production designer Michael White, a veteran of the Bruckheimer-produced films *The Rock* and *Crimson Tide*. "There were so many huge special and visual effects involved in this sequence that you couldn't really do it [the actual pyrotechnics] in downtown Manhattan," White notes, "so you bring Manhattan to downtown L.A. We shut down four city blocks in Los Angeles and for two to three weekends in a row brought in our mass destruction. L.A. is very film-friendly. It's the major industry here, so the town works with you."

In filmmaking terminology, *visual effects* is basically concerned with compositing—that is, layering—separately filmed elements into one seamless image or with creating 3-D characters and environments from the blank slate of the digital realm. (Visual effects people refer to this as CGI, for "computer-generated imagery.") By contrast, *special effects* works with physical props and pyrotechnics, producing effects live for the camera. To make the meteorite-hit sequence, production designers would integrate visual effects (the computer-generated images of rocks streaking through the sky, created by Computer Film Company) with special effects (the live-action explosions at point of impact).

"Blowing things up is exciting. It's a real rush, but it's also dangerous," says special-effects master John Frazier, whose company handled everything from building the Armadillo, the futuristic surface vehicle and drilling machine that Harry's doomsday squadron takes to the asteroid, to stirring up the debris that bedevils Armageddon's heroes on the asteroid's surface. "The big thing with pyrotechnics is not so much the final effect, which is pretty much worked out in advance, but making sure you know where something will land so nobody gets hurt."

Frazier tips his cap to a Ford Motor Company program that provides movie studios with unsaleable cars to trash. "Basically the whole thing was chaos," Frazier grins, recalling the dozens of cars catapulted, dropped, blown up, and smashed during the simulation of space-rock hits during the L.A. location work. "We launch the automobiles with what we call car flippers, pneumatic rams which are put underneath the cars. They can expend up to 1,200 pounds of pressure and flip a car 15 feet into the air. We also dropped a car suspended from a cable, so it spiraled down and hit the asphalt. One thing I suggested to Michael Bay was to have some fragments go horizontally through car windows and a bus."

Frazier, Jim Schwalm (Frazier's special effects foreman), and their crew weren't lighting detonation fuses with wild abandon. Such effects required extensive research at the L.A. site to scope out every possible angle, with still photos, video, storyboards, and miniature models helping plot the logistics. Achieving the desired level of carnage demanded that some hapless pedestrians also be thrown into the mix—which is where longtime Hollywood stunt coordinator Kenny Bates comes in.

Here's how Bates (whose other *Armageddon* duties included serving as the film's associate producer and second unit director) recalls a piece of the action: "We figured if a meteor could hit a bus it'd be great, but let's also have a car flying and twisting through the air with a stunt driver inside. We had one car flying 90 feet into the air and hitting the front of the bus, the back of the bus blows up, and I've got people everywhere—about 50 stunt people fleeing the scene. So much work goes into the logistics of that, just element after element."

Bates, whose recent credits include the Bruckheimer/Bay productions *Bad Boys* and *The Rock*, calls *Armageddon*'s "New York" meteor hit the biggest stunt sequence of his career. The prep work was designed to maximize the illusion of danger without risking the lives of the stunt performers. Thus, through a simple perspective trick effected by a certain camera angle, a flying, flaming car could plummet to earth seemingly only a few feet from a stunt performer—when in reality the crash occurred a safer 25 feet away. Beyond calculating the danger zone for explosions and flying objects, the choreography of controlled violence requires every stunt performer to hit his or her "mark," a spot on the ground that might be indicated by a simple Styrofoam cup or a chunk of burning debris.

"To prepare for a scene we'll do half-speed walk-throughs," Bates elaborates. "When it's blocked the way we want it, all the cues are correct, and we go to the action, my job is to make sure that in this whole insanity everything is performed safely and nobody gets hurt. There's always something that can go wrong. I have to catch those potential dangers and eliminate them so our stunt person is performing a calculated risk as opposed to a thrill-seeker making a daredevil stunt."

Bates' passion about the art of calculated risks comes from the many hazards inherent in his profession. "It's really demanding to try to make something as creative and dangerous as possible but with the least amount of risk," Bates says. "You dream about it at night. When you're shooting something like the downtown Los Angeles sequence, you wake up in the night screaming 'Go to your right, go to your right, don't stand

PRECEDING PAGES: *Scenes of turmoil as the first fiery pieces of the asteroid strike Manhattan.*

THIS PAGE: *Behind-the-scenes production photograph of the exploded bus ready to be finished off by a flaming car.*

there!' Very, very demanding job. We risk our lives many times. If you hit the wrong mark, if you're not up when the action starts and take a late cue, that can kill you. It's usually the little things that will kill you in this business."

The production's visual effects unit, which seamlessly integrated its own work with the live action, included an in-house shop of freelancers (dubbed "Vfx") headed by overall visual-effects supervisor Pat McClung (whose recent films include *Apollo 13* and *Dante's Peak*) and Richard Hoover at Disney's own Dream Quest Images. Other outfits handling some of the nearly 200 visual-effects shots were Computer Film Company (CFC), VIFX, and Pacific Ocean Post.

The creative freedom available with digital technology made it possible to stage the destruction of a piece of New York City. "Digital helps us open our boundaries," production designer White observes. "We can actually take our downtown L.A. footage, where you can see blue sky behind the buildings, and give it the density of New York by compositing into that space a 50- to 100-story skyline."

Visual effects work for the New York meteor-hit sequence began early on, with supervisor McClung and effects producer Thom Randmaa reading the script and flagging potential effects shots. In addition to the exploding cars, an early script revision called for a truck-sized projectile blasting through "three huge buildings." In the final version, visual effects creators would play with Big Apple iconography by having the meteor clip off the spire of the Chrysler Building, then blast through the Grand Hyatt Building and finally explode into Grand Central Station.

Building that shot was a long process, beginning with a New York location shoot by Vfx director of photography Philipp Timme and his crew. From a Manhattan rooftop, a sweeping camera traced the path of the imaginary meteor from the sky down through the Chrysler Building. This "background plate" footage (filmed with large-format 35-millimeter Vista Vision cameras) could then be scanned into a computer and the footage composited with other elements, ultimately creating the illusion of a single fantastic event.

One separately produced piece of film composited into the final image was of a "debris element" of the space rock smashing through the Chrysler Building, an effect created by using an air mortar to blow a concoction of dirt, miniature model girders, and other fragments through a "greenscreen," the neutral backdrop that effects artists use to isolate individual elements of the composite. "What you can do with greenscreen now is phenomenal," says Vfx project supervisor David Sanger. "You can extract just about anything, even things that used to be difficult or impossible, like smoke, as long as your film stock is good and your images are clear. Once we got all our elements together the plate went to Computer Film Company, which did some of our compositing work."

BELOW AND FAR RIGHT: *Original storyboards by Robbie Consing.*

RIGHT [AND FOLLOWING PAGES]: *Vfx computer-generated film footage of the Chrysler Building in mid-destruction.*

More than just computers were needed to realize the streaking meteor hit on film. The Vfx model department was involved as well, creating a model of the falling Chrysler Building and a pyrotechnic hit on a scale replica of a Grand Central Station frieze. The sequence of the Chrysler Building spire falling would require an initial view from the street—as the meteor severs the top of the skyscraper—and a punctuation point as the spire skewers the ground.

For the shot looking up at the Chrysler Building, Timme shot a variety of pan-and-tilt background plate moves with an encoded camera. After director Bay selected a final move, Timme was able to utilize the encoded data to duplicate the moves with a motion-control camera trained on a model. (Motion

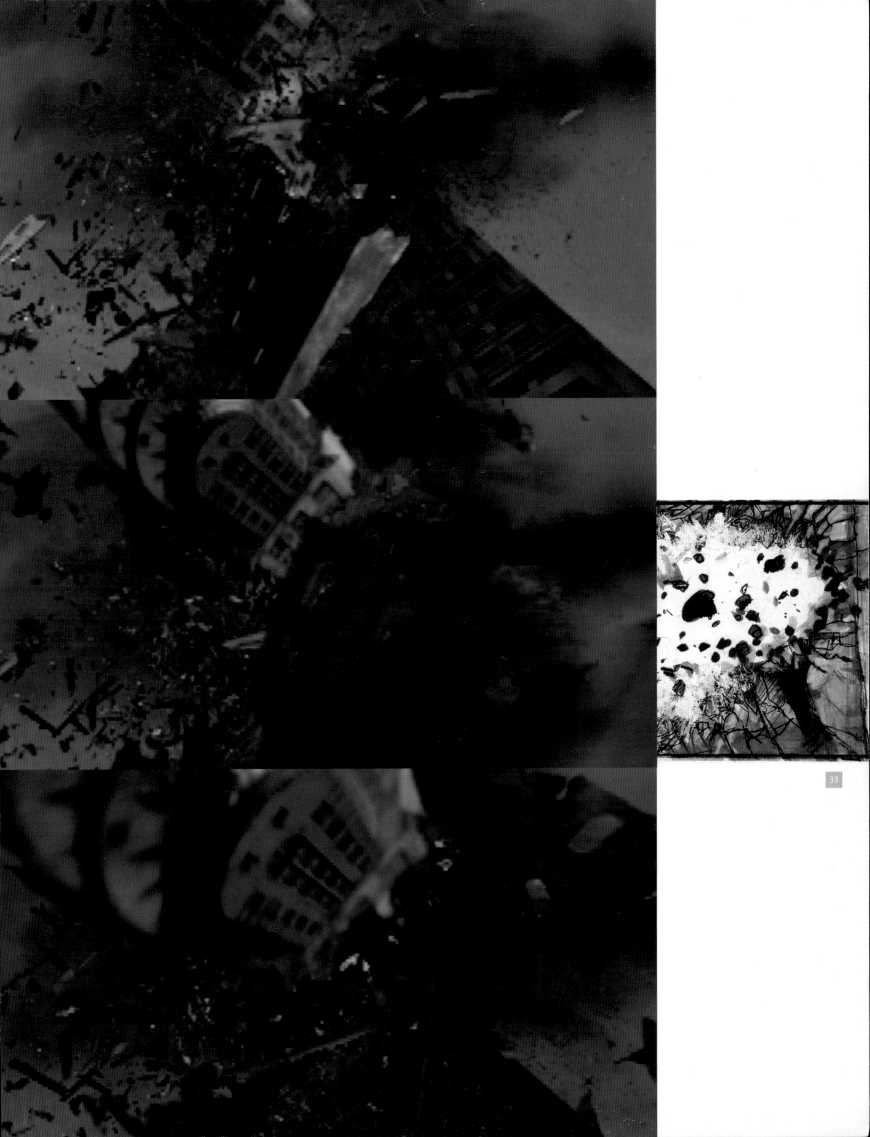

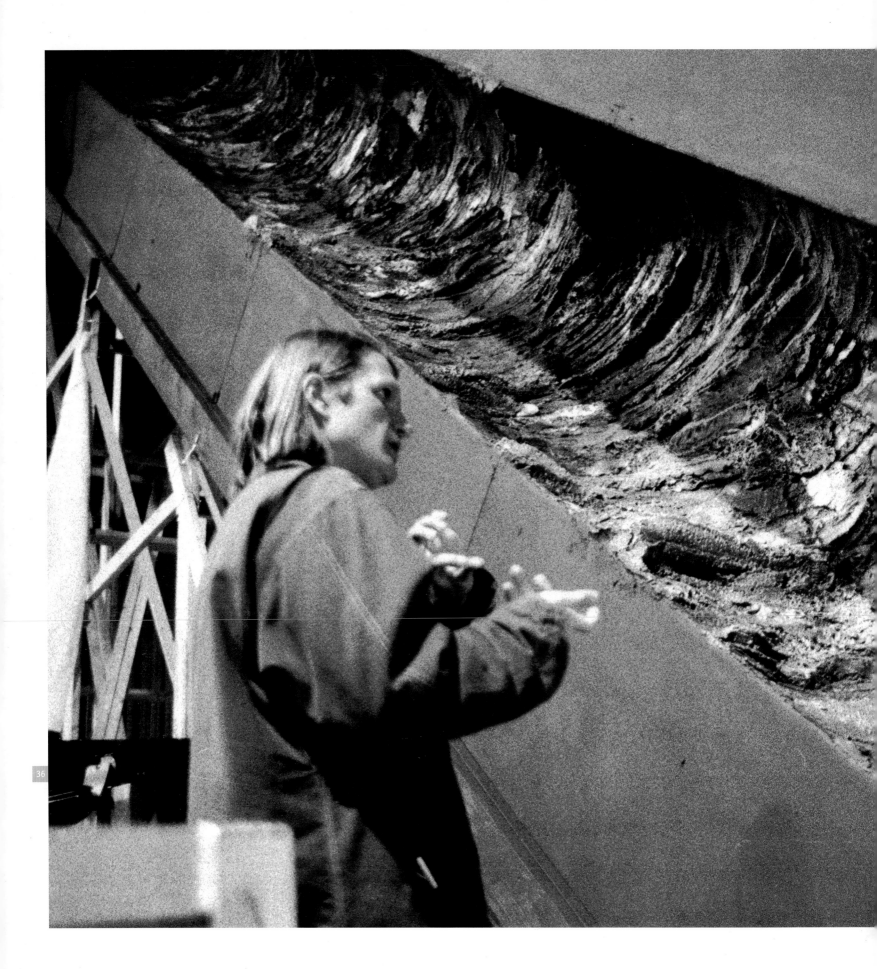

control is the computerized process that allows for the programming of specific, repeatable movements on cameras, models, and props.) The street view of the building would include placing the 1/40-scale model of the skyscraper's spire on a motion-control mount on an indoor greenscreen stage, then digitally incorporating that final element into footage of a "forced perspective" model of the rest of the building. This footage was shot outdoors, with Vfx model supervisor Alan Faucher's shop creating the forced-perspective building as a 17-foot-high structure, five feet wide at the base and tapering up to a two-foot width at the top.

Explaining the final shot—which also incorporates background photography shot in Manhattan—McClung says, "When the building hits the ground, it's a 1/24-scale, 16-foot long physical model. We literally dropped the model in front of a greenscreen we'd set up in our parking lot, shooting it with high-speed cameras."

The main *Armageddon* effects units at Vfx and Dream Quest would ultimately produce dozens of physical models for the show—quite a bonanza for the model-building craft, whose demise was predicted (prematurely, it turns out) with the advent of the computer-generated dinosaurs of 1993's *Jurassic Park*. "The fear was the computer would have replaced model-making within five years, and maybe it will in another ten years," says Alan Faucher. "But on this show I supervised the building of asteroid terrain and some 20 models, including two space shuttles and a Mir-type space station. What has happened is the computer is an enhancement tool. You can shoot a model, then digitally composite-in environments and subtle atmospheric effects that make it more believable and a much nicer blend with the first-unit live action."

Indeed, today's visual-effects techniques are no longer breakthroughs—they've just become a normal part of the moviemaking process. Computers allow visual-effects production teams to integrate fantastic visions seamlessly into the flow of a movie. "In the not-so-old days, you had to lock off your camera if you were shooting live-action that had to have a composite element in it," recalls McClung, an effects veteran from the "optical" days, when compositing was done on photochemical-based optical printers. "If you had a director with a moving camera style and you came to an effects shot, it'd be like the brakes were slammed on for the locked-off shot. Now, with the computer, you can integrate effects into moving shots and add realistic motion blur. Directors today have the freedom to do whatever they want."

But the new freedom doesn't make moviemaking any easier—it merely raises the creative bar with each movie. "As the technology increases so does the complexity of what directors want," Vfx's Sanger explains. "A director like Michael Bay, who likes dynamic shots and a wide range of action, really pushes the technology to its limits."

LEFT: *Production designer Michael White and director Michael Bay discuss the next setup in front of the ten-foot replica of the drilling hole.*

INSET: *Production designer Michael White.*

THE DIRECTOR

The typical Hollywood vehicle can get sidetracked along the labyrinthine trail of "development hell," that tangled pathway where ideas languish or are lost for years, even decades. But the process leading to *Armageddon*'s making was comparatively swift: Michael Bay estimates that the idea sprang to life—full-blown and high-concept—during the autumn of 1996. By February 1997, Bay's mentor Bruckheimer had come aboard, and within a year the production was wrapping the first-unit phase. By that time post-production—from completing visual effects to scoring the music—was in full swing, readying the film for its scheduled July 1, 1998, release.

Bay's own rise to the directorial elite seems meteoric. His first films, *Bad Boys* and *The Rock*, got the kind of big box-office that inspires bold headlines in the trades. Before turning to films, Bay had directed music videos and commercials, but his career had begun years before that, with a stint working for the Egg Company (the nearly forgotten L.A.-based outfit that established the Lucasfilm empire).

"I was fifteen and had my own office and phone at Egg. I was also the shortstop on their softball team. They'd done *Star Wars* and just finished *The Empire Strikes Back*. I remember having to file all the storyboards for this movie in production called *Raiders of the Lost Ark*. At the time I told all my friends, 'Yeah, Steven Spielberg is doing this movie—and it's really going to *suck!*'" Bay laughs, then continues: "Then I saw the movie at Grauman's Chinese Theater in Hollywood, and it's what inspired me to go into the movie business.

"I first did a lot of music videos and commercials, but that was to get my feet wet. I knew all along I was going to direct feature films. Critics think I'm a commercials director who just happened to get into movies, but it was a grand plan I had for a long time. I did *Bad Boys*—which had the charisma of the two stars [Will Smith and Martin Lawrence]—so I could be commercially successful and create my own destiny.

"Coming out of music videos and commercials, I learned how to shoot very quickly and also make something look good. One of my knacks is shooting for the edit, basically editing things in my mind. On *Bad Boys* I was working with a crew I hadn't worked with before and they probably thought I was crazy because I was putting cameras in weird places: 'It's not going to cut,' people said. But I'm just not traditional. I detail storyboards for action scenes but I also like to do a lot of improvising to get things that just magically happen. I love musicals. When you talk about filmmaking, that was the first type of movie to really exploit film as a medium. Musicals give the viewer privileged angles, they break the walls and do a lot of unorthodox things.

"I love the audience's enjoyment. It's the reason I make movies. The other great thing about doing movies is you get to be around things you never get to see in real life. You can say, 'I'd like to have this two-billion-dollar aircraft over here,' and they show it to you! But movies are all in the human emotion. You can have as much hardware as you want, but it has to be about character.

"It's funny, critics like to trash movies like *Armageddon*—but these are the movies that travel around the world the most. There's nothing wrong with entertaining audiences."

38

RIGHT: *Director Michael Bay.*

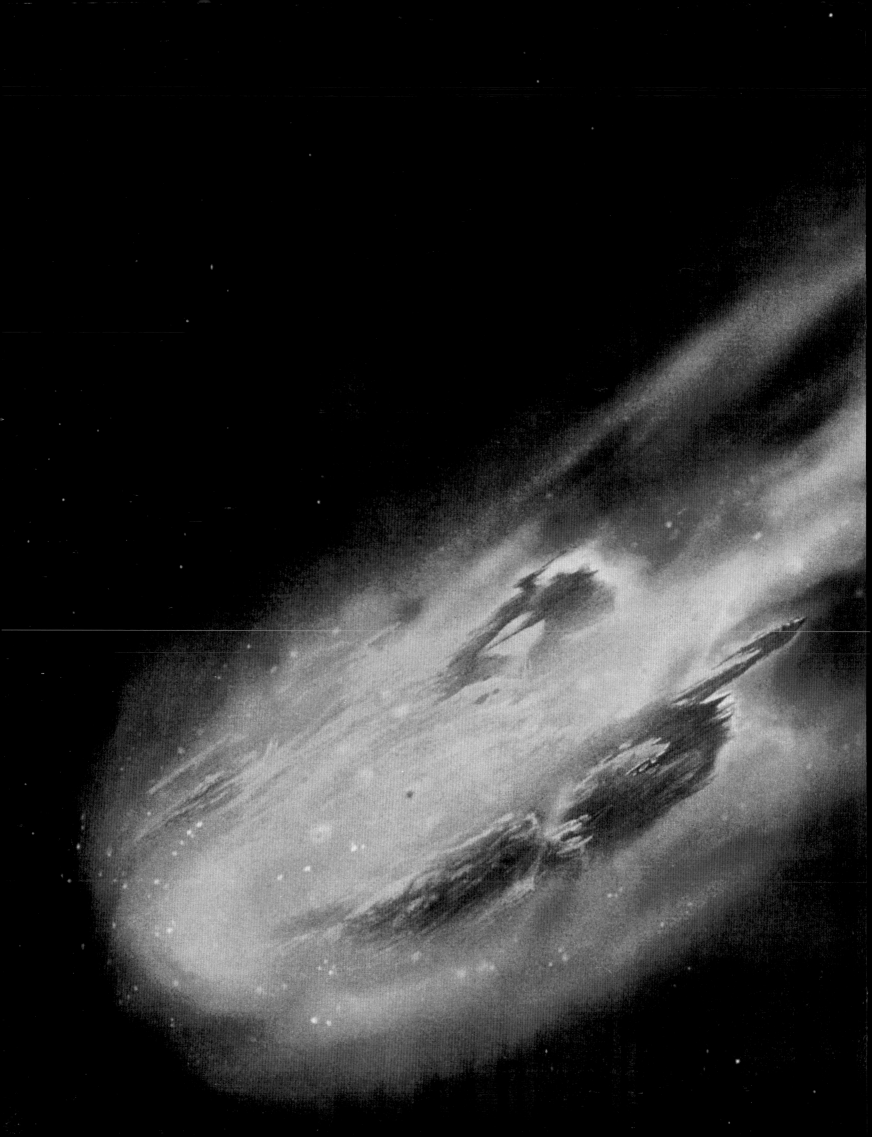

The genesis of *Armageddon* can be traced to a screenplay written by Robert
Pool in development at Disney, about a man with a foreboding of an apocalyp-
tic asteroid hit. Producer Gale Anne Hurd showed the script to Jonathan
Hensleigh, a corporate lawyer–turned–screenwriter whose second career had
already involved him with projects ranging from *Jumanji* to *The Rock* and *Con
Air*. And thus the doomsday-asteroid concept began gestating in their minds.

The doomsday scenario posed by *Armageddon* had already moved out of the
realm of fantasy on July 16, 1994, the date comet Shoemaker-Levy pulled into
the orbit of Jupiter, releasing 21 giant fragments that smashed into the planet
at an estimated 134,000 miles per hour. Then, in May 1996, that "global killer"
asteroid a third of a mile long came within a cosmic hairbreadth of Earth.

Most astonishing of all was the mile-sized asteroid spotted in December
1997 through the telescopic sights of the University of Arizona's Spacewatch
program. Astronomers around the world began tracking the orbit of the asteroid
(dubbed "Asteroid 1997 XF11"), with the sum of their calculations revealed on
March 11, 1998, by the Central Bureau for Astronomical Telegrams (the interna-
tional astronomical agency based at the Smithsonian Astrophysical Observatory
in Cambridge, Massachusetts). Their chilling conclusion: in the year 2028 the
asteroid would not only pass close to Earth (anywhere from half a million to a
scant 30,000 miles) but could conceivably crash into the planet, generating
global tidal waves, fires, and a nuclear winter effect from the eruption of debris
into the atmosphere. Scientists pinpointing and pondering calculations and
impact possibilities have, at this writing, offered up the idea of detonating a
nuclear device to knock the potential future global killer off its orbit—the same
course of action pursued by the heroes of *Armageddon*.

"There's always a basis in reality for an idea," Hurd notes. "If you buy into
the premise that Earth has been dramatically changed by comet and asteroid
strikes in the past, then clearly the most significant event that could happen in
our lifetimes—other than an extraterrestrial visitation—is the possibility of
being hit by an asteroid."

Michael Bay was looking for a good script when Hensleigh approached the
director with the idea that would become *Armageddon*. After months in which
Bay and Hensleigh developed the particulars of Hensleigh's "Eureka" inspiration,
the duo visited the office of Joe Roth for that venerable Hollywood ritual—the
"pitch" meeting. Roth, looking for a potential movie event for summer 1998,

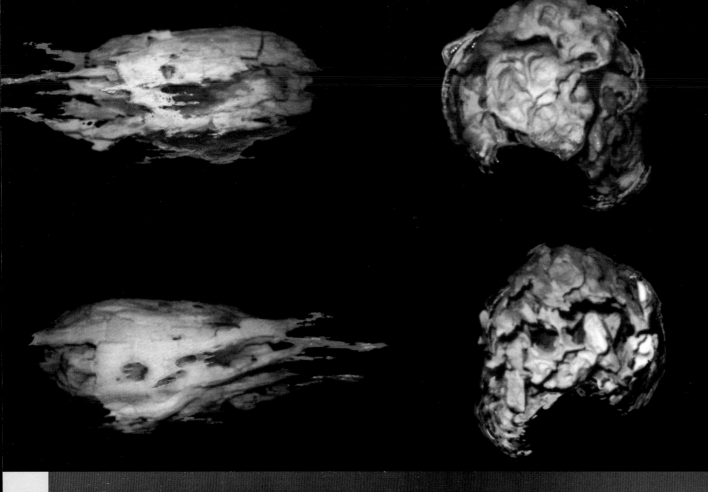

made the meeting a pitch to remember: not only did he greet the concept with enthusiasm, he even suggested "Armageddon" as the title. "The concept was almost green-lit from the pitch," Hurd recalls. "From that point it went to how quickly we could get a script together."

Beyond the doomsday premise, it was the character-conflict ideas that helped sell the project. "You always want to strive for a story that would be great even without larger-than-life things happening," Hurd says. "Before the crisis of this global killer starts you have a traditional story everyone can relate to. You have Harry Stamper, a guy who's made it single-handedly as the best oil-driller in the world. His world is full of tough guys, but it's not that glamorous. He wants a different life for his daughter. He doesn't want her to fall for someone that's like him—but that's what happens. She falls for his protégé, A. J. Frost. So the film has a great dramatic conflict on a human level."

Hensleigh describes his initial cracking of the asteroid premise as a "Eureka!" experience. While he mused about a potential storyline for the asteroid film, another idea he'd been mulling over for years was still percolating in his mind—this one about a roughneck oil-driller cut from the same mold as the real-life Red Adair, the famed oilfield firefighter. Years before, Hensleigh had jotted down an equation in his story-idea notebook: "Oil Driller = Red Adair = Harry Stamper." The fictional oil-driller's name was inspired by Pacific Northwest logger Hank Stamper, a character in Ken Kesey's novel *Sometimes a Great Notion*. Then came the flash of inspiration that matched a story to Harry Stamper.

"I was in the shower about five o'clock in the morning when the whole thing congealed into one film idea," Hensleigh remembers. "A lot of these big-budget Hollywood movies are based on the classic 'what if?'—in this case, what if NASA discovers that an enormous asteroid is hurtling towards Earth and they have the technology to get to the asteroid surface but they don't have the technology to drill and drop in the bomb that'll knock it off-course? Well, they have to rely—and here's the 'Eureka!' part—on Harry Stamper, the world's foremost deep-core driller, and his scruffy team. The entire story idea came together in that one moment. It was the ultra high-tech of NASA meets the ultra low-tech of the oil-drilling world. Michael Bay loved the idea of roughnecks in space."

"The story had big themes about underdogs and a seemingly impossible mission, yet also had the possibility of injecting humor in the midst of the most horrific crisis—those are the themes I personally

PRECEDING PAGES: *The final asteroid look would feature spiky, miles-long rock formations trailing the asteroid's tail. The asteroid was imagined as a real character—a totally evil presence. Dream Quest Images computer-generated art by Mike Meaker.*

PRECEDING PAGE INSET: *Two astronauts caught up in an explosion on the asteroid.*

ABOVE LEFT: *Dream Quest Images, assigned the task of creating asteroid elements for the visual effects work, hones in on the look the director wants in these 2½-foot asteroid maquettes.*

ABOVE RIGHT: *Star Ben Affleck [in the role of oil driller A.J. Frost] strikes a pose on the asteroid set.*

BOTTOM LEFT: *Chick Chapple [Will Patton].*

enjoy exploring," Bay says. "I enjoy drawing on the classic myths that have always been with us, which people anywhere on the planet can relate to. One of the great archetypes is the wise soul who teaches and empowers the young soul through a transforming journey. That's the central theme I explored in *Armageddon* with Bruce Willis and Ben Affleck."

The actual writing of the screenplay Hensleigh recalls as "full-bore mania," the likes of which he'd never before experienced professionally. The month of November 1996 was spent in a "crash course in astrophysics," with consultant Ivan Bekey detailing the basic science integral to the story. By the end of December, Hensleigh's creative fever had produced a first-draft script.

"Although this is a very cynical age," Hensleigh notes, "I know Michael was shooting for a picture in which America and the world are faced with certain death but people don't react by looting stores and killing each other—there's a unification of humanity, rather than a splitting apart."

The germination of the story began with four months of Hensleigh and Bay developing the pitch premise into a full-blown story. Then a number of writers working with Bay and Bruckheimer built on the script's first-draft foundation. While some journalists have derided such group scripting efforts, Bruckheimer notes that this has been the tradition since the glory era of the Hollywood studio system.

"In the heyday of the '30s and '40s scripts would start with an idea from one writer and a great plot writer would develop it, then a wonderful character writer would be called in or a female writer to script the female characters, someone to work on the dialogue, and even punch-up comedy writers might be added into the mix," Bruckheimer explains. "This has been going on forever. You always try to make things better. That's where different writers come in. We pinpoint the areas we feel need to be improved, and we'll talk ideas."

Bruckheimer recalls those *Armageddon* brainstorming sessions as a six-to-eight week preproduction marathon during which he, Bay, and the various writers talked through scenes to be rewritten or new concepts to be scripted. Even deep into the actual production calendar the scripters were still writing new scenes. Bay singles out for praise a core writing group that included Tony Gilroy, J. J. Abrams, Scott Rosenberg, Shane Solerno, Paul Attanasio, and Ann Biderman, with the esteemed Robert Towne (*Chinatown*, *Shampoo*) also contributing.

Each screenwriter's unique perspective helped expand the world of *Armageddon*. For example, Hensleigh developed overall story structure, while Gilroy tweaked this structure and embellished the individual personalities of Harry and his roughnecks through a doomsday mission recruitment and training period as well as a prelaunch night out (during which one roughneck lavishes loan shark–borrowed funds on a favorite stripper while another pays a poignant visit to his ex-wife to see his son). Rosenberg added a deeper dimension to the love story of Grace and A.J., including the so-called "Animal Crackers" scene, an interlude—written during production—in which A.J. toys with some animal cookies on Grace's stomach. It's a "silly kind of thing that provides a sweet moment in the movie," says Bay.

Sometimes an idea misfired, which is what happened to an early draft by Shane Salerno, a young, eager scriptwriter who rewrote some 50 pages in three days. "Shane's rewrite opened up with the death of the dinosaurs, which had always been there, and a fairly long opening about a pregnant woman with the Spacewatch program who was trying to figure out what to name her kid," Bay recalls. "It wasn't quite what I had in mind. You have to grab the audience in the first 30 seconds or they'll walk out of the theater, so he reworked that opening and came up with this brilliant idea of going from 65 million years ago to the present day, with little meteorites ripping through the wings of the orbiting space shuttle and blowing it up. We've never lost anybody in actual outer space, so that was also a brilliant way of introducing and making an emotional connection with the character of NASA head Dan Truman, who makes it a personal mission to stop this oncoming asteroid."

The road to *Armageddon*, which began with Hensleigh's inspiration in the shower, and the screenwriter and director developing the idea in concept, ultimately benefited from producer Jerry Bruckheimer's contribution and the other voices that punched up and polished a final script. "A movie is such a collaborative effort," Bay concludes. "I like having other writers look at a script. Making a movie involves so many different types of people and life experiences. Each writer has something to add. Sometimes they go off in wrong directions—and sometimes they bring back gems."

LEFT, TOP TO BOTTOM: *Top row: Walt Disney Studios chairman Joe Roth and star Bruce Willis. Second row: Screenwriter Jonathan Hensleigh, producer Jerry Bruckheimer, and director Michael Bay. Third row left: Sound mixer Keith Wester. Third row right/top: Walt Disney Motion Pictures Group chairman Dick Cook and producer Jerry Bruckheimer. Third row right/bottom: Second assistant director Jeff Okabayashi, director Michael Bay, and special effects foreman Jim Schwalm. Fourth row left: Script supervisor Karen Golden and producer Jerry Bruckheimer. Fourth row right: Screenwriter Jonathan Hensleigh and producer Gale Anne Hurd. Bottom: Director Michael Bay and his crew.*

ABOVE: *Director Michael Bay checks the angle of his Panaflex Platinum.*

RIGHT: *left to right: Director of photography John Schwartzman, director Michael Bay, and gaffer Andy Ryan contemplate the asteroid set.*

310 | 37 | 40:20
HRS | MIN | SEC MSEC

PART TWO

THE DOOMSDAY
SQUADRON

"They just asked me to save the world.
You really think I'm gonna say 'No'?"

—*Harry Stamper (from the* Armageddon *script)*

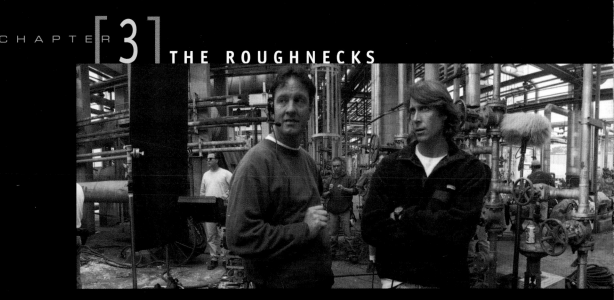

Red Adair, the real-life inspiration for Harry Stamper, could size up and cap any oil fire. In 1962, in the Algerian Sahara, Red used 550 pounds of dynamite to cap a pillar of flame gushing 450 feet (a feat that earned "Greatest Gas Fire" distinction in the *Guinness Book of Records*) while 30 years later Adair and his men were among the crews bringing under control the Kuwaiti oil fields set ablaze at the end of the 1991 Gulf War. Five-foot-six, with a stocky wrestler's build, Adair has been called "an American hero," the personification of rugged individualism and two-fisted determination—the kind of guy who, if the world were on the line, might even take on an asteroid.

NO CUSSING
STAMPER OIL

As with its meticulous research on asteroids and space travel, the *Armageddon* production team would do its homework on Harry Stamper's oil-drilling world. "A drill site is low-tech and dangerous," Bay says. "There are only a few great oil drillers in the world that go down 80,000 feet into the earth. It's a whole different world, with its own lingo. One of Harry's crew, Rockhound, played by Steve Buscemi, is an unconventional but brilliant geologist. You watch these guys moving 90-foot pieces of pipe with tongs and it's like a dance, so second-nature they barely look at each other as they pass off that pipe. Their hands are so close to this big claw that clamps down on the pipe—they could lose their hands so easily!

"I had my office try to find the best oil drillers in the world, the whole idea being we wanted to find a character who's like Red Adair," Bay adds. "We found a guy named Jon Marshall, who's got a ton of oil rigs, and we went to Texas to meet him. We're out on a rig off the coast somewhere, it's dinner and we're eating our steaks, and we asked Marshall what he thought about the idea of oil drillers going up to an asteroid to save the planet. 'Naw,' he goes, 'wouldn't work. Gravity.' He gives me all the logical stuff. But one of the reasons we made the asteroid the size of Texas is so it'd have a gravity, like the Moon. Also, we didn't think audiences would believe something just three miles across could actually wipe out life on Earth."

The character of Harry Stamper was a good fit for veteran action star Bruce Willis, whose lean and rugged looks were complemented by enough experience to project the stoic authority of the ultimate roughneck who's seen it all. "He's got a great sense of humor which really keeps the crew going," says Bay.

"Bruce is a really kind man," says Liv Tyler, the 19-year-old actress who plays Harry's daughter, Grace. "He helped the crew get off a couple days earlier for the Christmas holidays. It was interesting to watch the way he handles himself. He's a pro."

PRECEDING PAGES: *Top right: First assistant director K. C. Hodenfield and director Michael Bay at the abandoned refinery that stands in for the Stamper Oil Company deep-sea oil rig. Bottom: Behind the scenes at Edwards Air Force Base, where the Stealth Bomber was first allowed to be filmed for a motion picture.*

LEFT: *Bruce Willis as Harry Stamper.*

ABOVE: *One of Stamper Oil's Golden Rules.*

RIGHT: *Harry goes on a rampage when he finds A.J. with his beloved daughter, Grace. At right is Charles "Chick" Chapple (played by Will Patton), who keeps a wary eye on the situation, while Rockhound (Steve Buscemi) looks nonplussed in the background.*

PRECEDING
PAGES: Rockhound mans the fort
at Stamper Oil.

THIS PAGE: A.J. Frost [Ben
Affleck].

TOP RIGHT: Jayotis "Bear"
Kurleen [Michael "Big Mike" Duncan].

BOTTOM RIGHT: Rockhound
[Steve Buscemi].

Chick Chapple, Harry's best buddy and right-hand man, is played by Will Patton. "Chick is one of the older guys, although I never thought I'd be saying I was one of the older guys," cracks Patton, whose past roles include parts in such noted films as *No Way Out*, *The Spitfire Grill*, and *The Postman*. "My character and Harry's character are so close they know each other without having to say anything because of all the time and secrets shared together."

In the film, the audience meets Harry and his crew at a "Stamper Oil Company" rig in the middle of the sea. Although extensive scenes were filmed at an abandoned oil refinery in Carson, California, early in the production, shooting at a real rig was still a priority, particularly for the dramatic scene in which a military helicopter arrives to pick up an unsuspecting Stamper and take him to the Johnson Space Center in Houston for a doomsday briefing.

After approaching four oil companies, technical adviser Marshall managed to elicit the support of David Henderson, the president of EEX Corporation, who let the *Armageddon* team use—gratis—an EEX semisubmersible oil rig in the Gulf of Mexico, 100 miles off the coast of Galveston, Texas. "This location was really important because we not only wanted to show a rig befitting the world's best deep-core driller, we wanted to sell the fact that they're really out in the middle of the ocean," says executive producer Jim Van Wyck. "This oil rig also tied in very well with the refinery we'd shot earlier. The rig was about eight stories high, out in the middle of the water. It could sleep 110 people, so myself and the crew slept on the rig and the cast went back and forth by helicopter."

From oil rigs to Air Force hangars, the production would find itself enthusiastically received—with the unprecedented access at NASA being the crowning touch in the opinion of many *Armageddon* insiders. "I think the credits for the movies I've done in the past kind of greased the way to get us in there," Bruckheimer muses. "They know we're not going to make them look bad. We can glamorize just about anything and make it look interesting."

Beyond the crowd-pleasing action of Bruckheimer productions like *Top Gun* is an unabashed patriotism that appeals to two-fisted oil drillers, fighter pilots, and NASA astronauts alike. "I love American ingenuity, and *Armageddon* is about that," Bruckheimer says. "The never-say-die, can-do attitude that if there's a problem we can figure out a way to solve it. That's how this country was built. That's the attitude that said we could put a man on the Moon. I think the whole space program is the realization of the American dream."

56

RIGHT: *Producer Jerry Bruckheimer and star Bruce Willis review the day's script pages.*

FOLLOWING PAGES: *Among the many responsibilities of Michael White's art department was coming up with a look for the spacesuits Harry and the roughnecks would be wearing for their mission. A special concern for the production was avoiding the puffy, inflated look of a real spacesuit. Helmet concept art by Jim Carson. Insets: At top spacesuit design concept art by James Oxford; middle, spacesuit concept art by Jim Carson; bottom, rear view of spacesuit design concept art by James Oxford, showing oxygen tank.*

James Oxford
6·15·97
SPACE SUIT

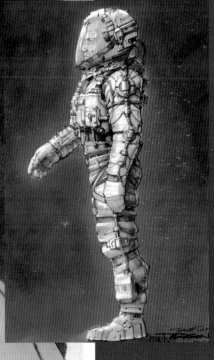

HELMET CONCEPT S

J. CARSON 4-

ARMAGEDDON

ARMAGEDDON
SPACE SUIT
JAMES OXFOR
6·25·97

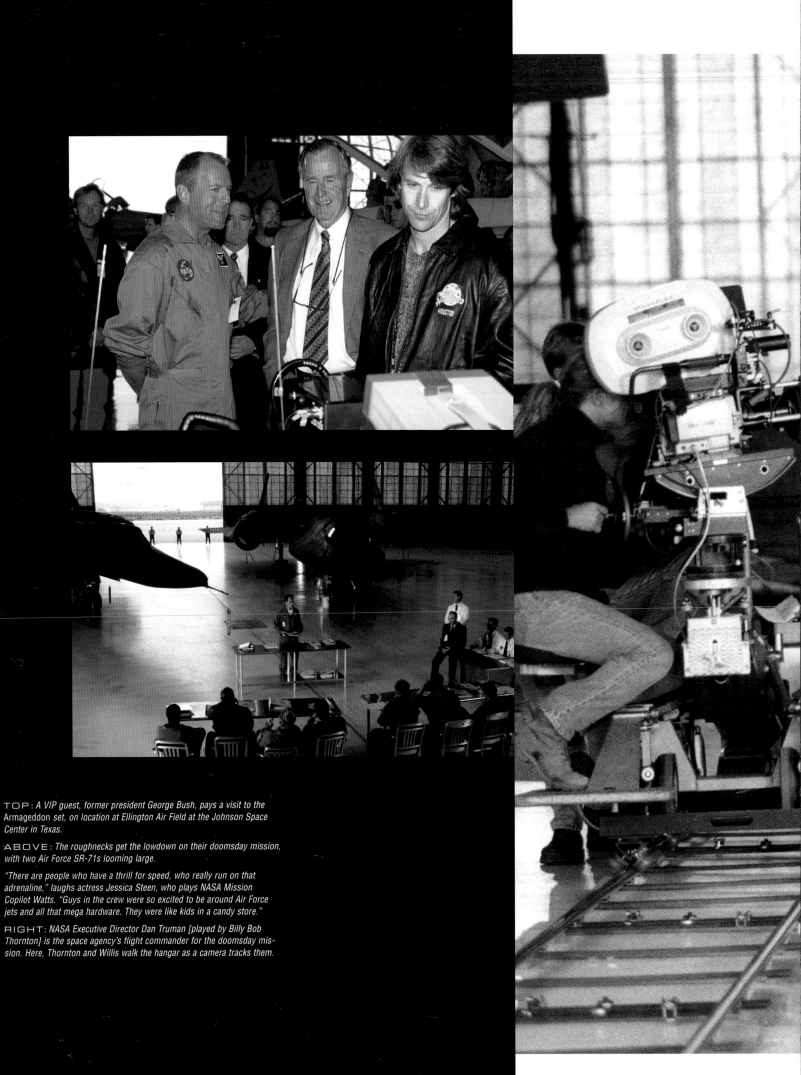

TOP: *A VIP guest, former president George Bush, pays a visit to the* Armageddon *set, on location at Ellington Air Field at the Johnson Space Center in Texas.*

ABOVE: *The roughnecks get the lowdown on their doomsday mission, with two Air Force SR-71s looming large.*

"There are people who have a thrill for speed, who really run on that adrenaline," laughs actress Jessica Steen, who plays NASA Mission Copilot Watts. "Guys in the crew were so excited to be around Air Force jets and all that mega hardware. They were like kids in a candy store."

RIGHT: *NASA Executive Director Dan Truman [played by Billy Bob Thornton] is the space agency's flight commander for the doomsday mission. Here, Thornton and Willis walk the hangar as a camera tracks them.*

ABOVE: *Colonel Sharp [William Fichtner] and Lieutenant Gruber [Grayson McCouch] prepare the final nuclear device for detonation on the asteroid.*

INSET: *Concept art for the nuclear bomb by Jim Carson.*

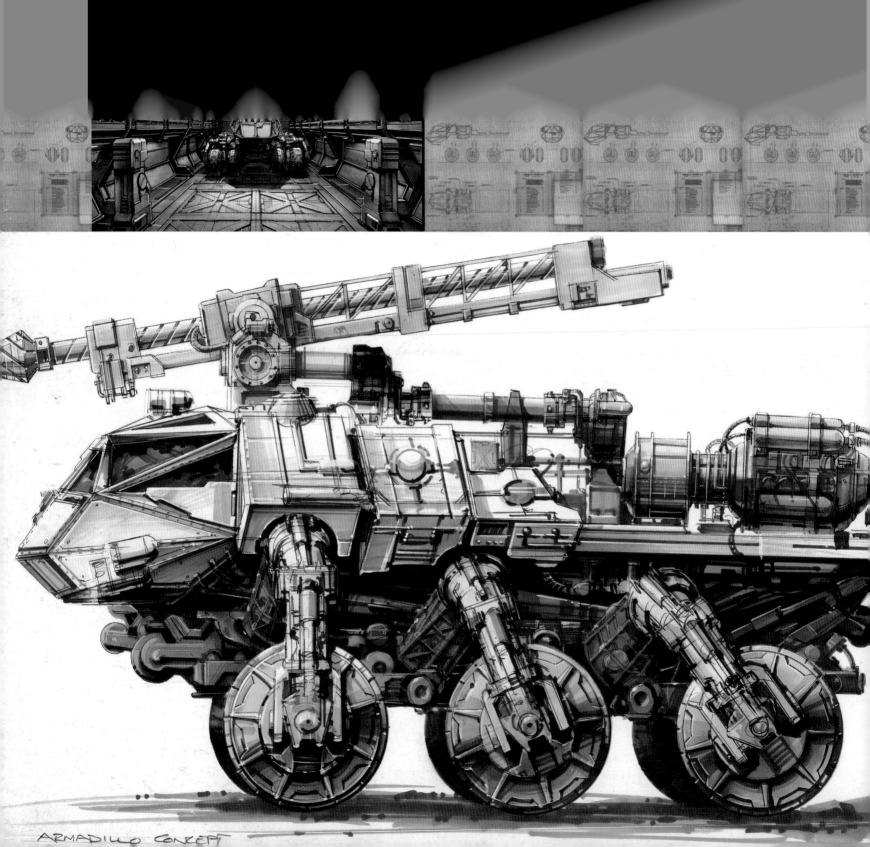

ARMADILLO CONCEPT

ASSYMETRICAL
LIGHT RACK?

GOTLIN / PHALANX
GUN TO FEND OFF
SMALL DEBRI

[P]OTENTIAL "METAL
[L]OOK" FUNCTIONAL
[R]UBBER TIRES OR
[A]CTUAL METAL
[P]LATES

OUTER WHEEL SUSPENSION
ARMS. ADD-ONS

ARMADILLO CONCEPT
J. CARSON 5-16-97
ARMAGEDDON

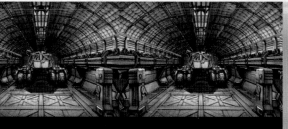

OPPOSITE: *Art department concept sketch of Armadillo, side view. Illustration by Jim Carson. Inset by James Oxford and blueprints by Kevin Ishioka.*

TOP: *Art department concept sketch of Armadillo, front view. Illustration by Jim Carson; and blueprints by Kevin Ishioka.*

ABOVE: *The Armadillo gets a test run in the Mojave Desert outside Edwards Air Force Base.*

According to designer Michael White, the Mars Pathfinder *mission's six-wheeled Sojourner robot inspired the multiwheel design of the Armadillo. [A far cry from the golf cart–like vehicles that traveled on the surface of the Moon, this giant vehicle would be fully encapsulated.] John Frazier says that in engineering the mechanics of something like the Armadillo he has to find out from the director what it's supposed to do, and then proceed accordingly. "It's got to work first, then we can make it pretty," Frazier grins.*

The specs on the Armadillo, built by Frazier's 50-person crew within two months: A gasoline-powered, four-wheel-drive vehicle with an exterior view area to allow for a designated driver; solid components from one end to the other; a Humvee chassis; and independent suspension wheels. [The 12 wheels were exclusively made by Goodyear from molds supplied by the production.]

ABOVE LEFT: *A.J. rides 'em high as a driller welds a section of the Armadillo.*

ABOVE RIGHT: *"Bear" welds away.*

BOTTOM RIGHT: *Stunt coordinator/second unit director Kenny Bates (lower left corner) directs Ben Affleck (hanging from harness) in this stunt sequence, as the Armadillo is hoisted into position for a green-screen shot.*

THIS PAGE: *The Space Shuttle Launch Pad at Kennedy Space Center, Cape Canaveral, Florida.*

TOP RIGHT: *Rockhound, Chick, Harry, A.J., and Bear prepare themselves for the launch.*

BOTTOM RIGHT: *The production at the shuttle launchpad area. "This movie was very complicated because we went to so many locations and had to pull off the technical side like clockwork," explains director of photography Schwartzman. "When you get access to shoot the space shuttle and launchpad you have a brief period of time and you have to adhere to all the standards NASA sets up while still accomplishing the things you want to achieve."*

"I remember when we got up on the gantry of the shuttle I asked for a cellphone," laughs actor William Fichtner. "I called my mom. 'Mom! You can't believe where I am!'"

"For *Armageddon*, I tried to bring back astronauts as heroes," Bay explains. "I grew up with all that Moon stuff but ever since the *Challenger* shuttle blew up [in 1986] the space program had lost some of its luster.

"It's hard to explain, but when you go and see NASA it's so patriotic! On the VIP tour you walk the walk the astronauts take to the shuttle. You go through the white room that leads to the shuttle—and then you're on the gantry and the shuttle is just sitting there, this huge ship that's loaded with a four-million-gallon fuel tank and has 270,000 moving parts that all have to work together."

Bay says that without NASA's cooperation *Armageddon* might not have been made. After all, Harry, A.J., Rockhound, and the rest of the roughnecks couldn't just be suited up and shot into space. Even with the doomsday clock ticking, Harry and the boys had to undergo a rigorous—though accelerated—training period to prepare for space flight. The chance to film the NASA training scenes, and ultimately an actual launch segment, at the space agency's own facilities (from the Johnson Space Center in Houston to the shuttle launch site at Kennedy Space Center in Florida) was a producer's dream come true.

Interestingly, the production discovered that the space agency—despite its high-tech reputation—wasn't some techno-Oz. "You think 'astronauts,' they fly up into space and walk around on the Moon," says production designer Michael White, "but when you visit NASA you realize it's hardware and crescent wrenches and nuts and bolts. They don't have some magic formula, they're just faced with a different set of problems to solve. It's what they accomplish with their tools. Every single mission is a triumph! We saw the result of one error, when the *Challenger* exploded after liftoff. So their tolerance level is zero."

The utilitarian aspect of NASA was particularly evident in the little touches: a piece of acoustic ceiling tile askew, the glare of government buildings lit in "early bureaucrat" harshness. Even Mission Control in Houston didn't have the eye-candy appeal a movie audience might expect from a control room coordinating the operations of spaceships and astronauts. "Films are very visual these days, from production and set designs to visual effects," White notes, "so you can't, on this type of action adventure film, just replicate reality."

Despite the utilitarian look of many of its facilities, NASA's gigantic scale was everything the production team had hoped for, from rocket thrusters that dwarf human beings to the vast underwater tank in which astronauts train for the weightless conditions of space—"the real deal," in the awed words of John Schwartzman, who as director of photography led his crew in lighting and filming all the first-unit work. "Everything is 'land of the giants' there. One of the places we shot was the Vehicle Assembly Building in Florida, where they assembled the Saturn V rocket which went to the Moon and where they now stack the space shuttle. It's the largest interior volume in the world—you could put Yankee Stadium on its roof!

"But NASA's buildings are lit for working, not for dramatics," Schwartzman adds. "Every place we went we basically had to relight. Their buildings are lit very industrial, they look more 1950s and we wanted to make them 1990s. We basically 'sexed up the place,' as Michael would say, providing lighting that created some modeling and depth yet still kept the space program's integrity, as if it had been lit by NASA."

INSET

BELOW: *All eyes at NASA Mission Control are on the video feed from outer space.*

The film's NASA Mission Control set had to marry the authenticity of the space agency with the dramatic license required for a big-budget action adventure. "When I worked on Apollo 13, special effects supervisor Ron Howard wanted us to make it look as real as possible," notes visual effects supervisor Pat McClung. "This film is different—Michael Bay wanted fantastic action and adventure."

"The Mission Control we built is what NASA would build if they could," laughs production designer Michael White. "But while ours does look better, their Mission Control works!"

"The Mission Control has a sparkle and pizzazz NASA doesn't have—mainly it's bigger," says NASA consultant Joe Allen, who worked in the real control room during the Apollo years, notably as a "capsule communicator" with the flight director for Apollo flights 15 and 17. "If what happens in the movie were to occur, it would be one critical thing after the other. People in the control room would be very alert and intense, and I think the filmmakers did a good job of capturing that feeling."

INSET: *Grace Stamper, Flight Director Walter Clark, General Kimsey, Harry Stamper, Executive Director of NASA Dan Truman outside the Johnson Space Center building near Houston.*

To transform NASA's workplace environments into Hollywood-caliber shooting stages, Schwartzman and his camera and lighting crews had to contend with that awe-inspiring scale. "To light something like the Vehicle Assembly Building you basically get every light in the world," Schwartzman laughs, only half-kidding. "That building is 65 stories tall, so you just go up to each different level—there are catwalks everywhere. We did have to use one-ton transformers because the power in the building wasn't right. Luckily, they have these incredibly large construction cranes that'll handle 400 tons, so it wasn't a problem to have one of our transformers lifted up to the 500-foot level. It took a good week to pre-rig that location, all for just 40 seconds of screen time. That's a lot of what NASA was—enormous amounts of rigging to pull these shots off."

73

TOP LEFT: *Producer Jerry Bruckheimer discusses a scene with Billy Bob Thornton, who plays Dan Truman, at the Mission Control set. Built on a stage at the Culver Studios, Mission Control was only one of the numerous locations needed for a production on the scale of* Armageddon.

MIDDLE LEFT: *Grace reflects on the enormity of the situation.*

BOTTOM LEFT: *Keith David is the top Air Force commander, General Kimsey.*

ABOVE: *Dan Truman barks out a command.*

PRECEDING PAGES : *At left, complete submersion—Bruce Willis [pictured] and Ben Affleck were the first civilians allowed access to Johnson Space Center's Neutral Buoyancy Lab. Active-duty astronauts assisted Willis and Affleck in their hour-long dives. At right, Willis is prepared to take the plunge in the NASA neutral buoyancy tank that simulates the weightless conditions astronauts face in space. Willis and Affleck were allowed a total of four hours in the world's largest indoor pool.*

BELOW : *Underwater in NASA's Weightless Environment Training Facility tank. NASA consultant Joe Allen gave both Willis and Affleck high marks for their work at the space agency training facility.*

RIGHT : *Affleck, out of the pool, takes a breather.*

FOLLOWING PAGES : *As time counts down to launch, the roughnecks and astronauts gather in the Hyperbaric Chamber for one last meeting before they face an onslaught of press. This chamber is located in the O & C Building at Kennedy Space Center and was used for training the Apollo astronauts. It is now used for training technicians who load experiments into the Space Lab modules.*

One of the highlights of the NASA shoot was the filming of Bruce Willis and Ben Affleck, garbed in spacesuits, taking a dive in the Weightless Environment Training Facility at the Johnson Space Center. This "neutral buoyancy tank" is a vast pool, 200 feet long by 100 feet wide, with "the clearest water you've ever seen," recalls executive producer Van Wyck. In the pool, astronauts—who are hooked up to cables that pump a nitrogen-oxygen combination into their suits—descend, plunging to a depth of some 40 feet, where there are full-scale mockups of shuttle and space-station sections. Accompanied by teams of scuba divers, the astronauts train here, in working conditions that approximate what they'll encounter in space. Getting *Armageddon* cameras at the site—and actors into the pool—was the toughest red tape to cut, according to Van Wyck.

"We were real fortunate to run into Ron Farris, the gentleman who runs that lab," Van Wyck explains. "We told him that in a perfect world we wanted to put Bruce Willis and Ben Affleck into their real ten-million-dollar spacesuits and take them underwater. They'd never had a civilian in a suit and underwater before. But Ron and his team were amazing—they fought a lot of battles for us."

Not only did Farris secure permission to suit up the stars for underwater filming (Willis and Affleck wore suits that had been through spaceflight), but Affleck was thrown into the mix with real astronauts. "We were allowed to film topside as all the astronauts and scuba divers were below," Van Wyck recalls, "and they were doing what they call an emergency egress, in which they simulate a problem and take one diver out. Ron got the idea that instead of putting the other diver back in after the emergency egress, why not put in one of our guys who was already suited up, in this case Ben Affleck? So, instead of just having Ben underwater with some scuba divers, we had him with [about seven] real astronauts, including Shannon Lucid [who spent an American-record 188 days on space aboard the *Mir* space station]. We have a wide shot of all these people underwater, and we move right into a priceless close-up on Ben."

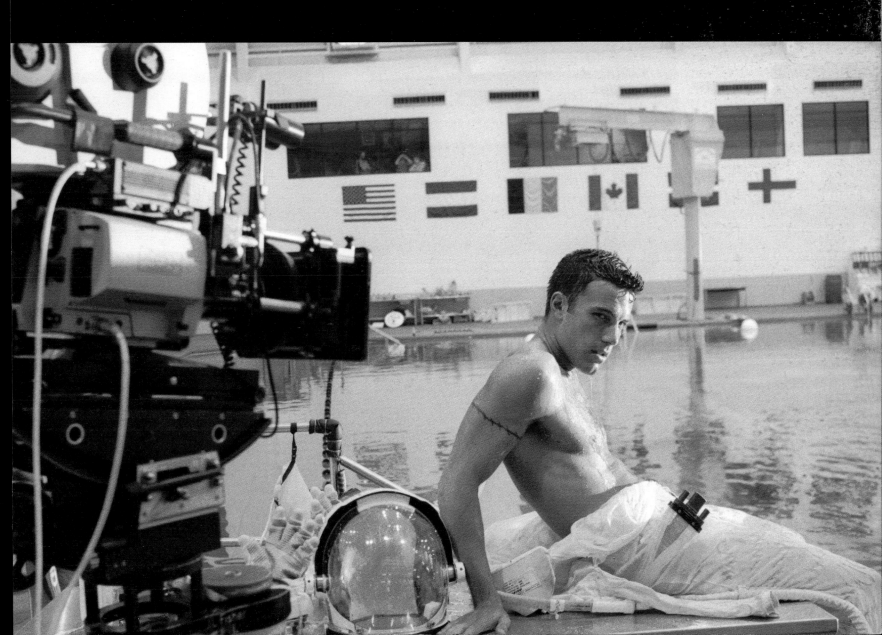

ABOVE: Independence *Shuttle crew patch design by Michael White and illustrated by Edwin Natividad.*

LEFT: *Anthony Guidera plays Copilot Tucker.*

CENTER: *Owen Wilson plays Oscar Choi.*

BOTTOM: *Greg Collins is Lieutenant Halsey.*

BELOW: *Peter Stormare is Lev Andropov, the Russian cosmonaut.*

ABOVE: *Ben Affleck is A.J. Frost.*

TOP RIGHT: *Actor Michael Clark Duncan plays Jayotis "Bear" Kurleen.*

CENTER RIGHT: *Marshall Teague plays Colonel Davis.*

BOTTOM RIGHT: *Clark Brolly plays Noonan.*

Advising the production on the veracity of everything from the proper mood of the Mission Control team to the push-the-envelope shuttle designs the movie unveils was Joe Allen, a former astronaut and currently chairman of Veridian, a transportation technology company. Allen's NASA career spanned the two worst American mishaps of the Space Age: he joined the agency just six months after the disastrous 1967 *Apollo* 1 launchpad fire that killed astronauts Virgil ("Gus") Grissom, Edward White, and Roger Chaffee; though Allen retired in 1985, he had been "cycling into a shuttle flight" set for early 1986 when the shuttle *Challenger*, barely a minute into its tenth orbital mission, exploded in the Florida sky. "Both were tragedies," Allen says softly. "The one happened during the Cold War, and during a war you lose good people. NASA investigated it and fixed it. The *Challenger* only required a minor modification to the solid rocket, but it was three years before we had the nerve to try it [a shuttle launch] again."

Allen did fly two shuttle missions, notably the 1984 *Discovery* flight in which he spacewalked twice, each time for an eight-hour session. The assignment for Allen, and his partner, Dale Gardener, was to retrieve two errant satellites, and on one of Allen's walks he was untethered, moving with the aid of a "rocket pack." Theirs was the only successful such retrieval mission to date, according to Allen. The satellites were brought back to Earth for refurbishment and were relaunched—and are still in orbit today. As a spacewalker, Allen knew what Willis and Affleck had gone through to get into their spacesuits.

"I was at the tank when they were suited up, and I was very impressed with both actors," Allen says. "They did it without much training, and they were under with active-duty astronauts, each of whom I know very well, and all were complimentary about how those guys did. It's very claustrophobic in the suit because when they snap the helmet on you can't touch your face and body. A spacesuit is inflated to three pounds of pressure per square inch, so when you move the volume changes. That takes energy, and after a while your limbs can get very tired.

"When you're in a suit and out in space it's virtually silent. On the '84 *Discovery* mission I became one of only four [astronauts] to go untethered in space, flying the Manned Maneuvering Unit—what they call the 'rocket pack,' a backpack with arms that come in front of you with controls on each arm. It's extraordinary, a three-dimensional magic carpet ride. You're floating in the suit like a creature in a cocoon, and the suit itself is floating around you. Intellectually you know you're going at 18,000 miles per hour. You yourself are a satellite."

LEFT: *The Anechoic Chamber (or vacuum chamber) at Johnson Space Center, which simulates gravitational conditions in space.*

RIGHT: *Here in the vacuum chamber training facility, astronauts and technicians test various pieces of equipment under a wide range of atmospheric conditions.*

BELOW: *Grace and A.J. find a place to be alone in a bigger-than-life piece of NASA hardware—the original Saturn 5 rocket thrusters [on display at the Kennedy Space Center Museum].*

RIGHT: *Liv Tyler is Grace Stamper.*

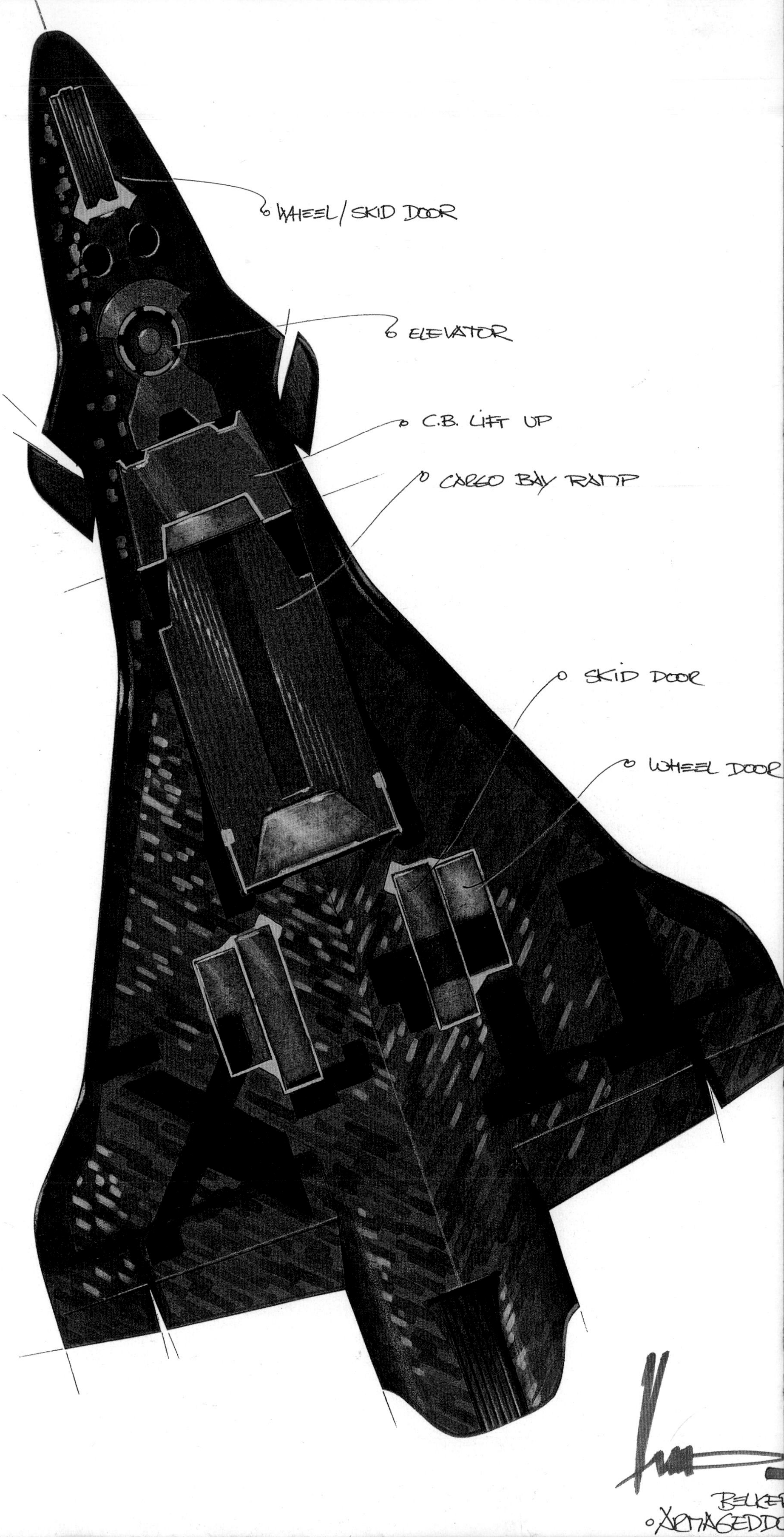

WHEEL/SKID DOOR

ELEVATOR

C.B. LIFT UP

CARGO BAY RAMP

SKID DOOR

WHEEL DOOR

RIGHT: *The doomsday mission will involve two teams divided into two shuttles, each a class "X-71"—the impossibly huge, impossibly advanced" space shuttle described in the original script.*

Art department study for the space shuttle by Wil Rees.

OPPOSITE TOP AND BOTTOM: *X-71 space shuttle design and detail of thrusters. Art department concepts by Wil Rees.*

INSET LEFT: *Spacesuit storage area in lower shuttle cargo bay. Art department illustration by James Oxford.*

INSET CENTER: *John Frazier [on ladder] and his special effects crew ready the shuttle set.*

INSET RIGHT: *Shuttle airlock. Art department illustration by James Oxford.*

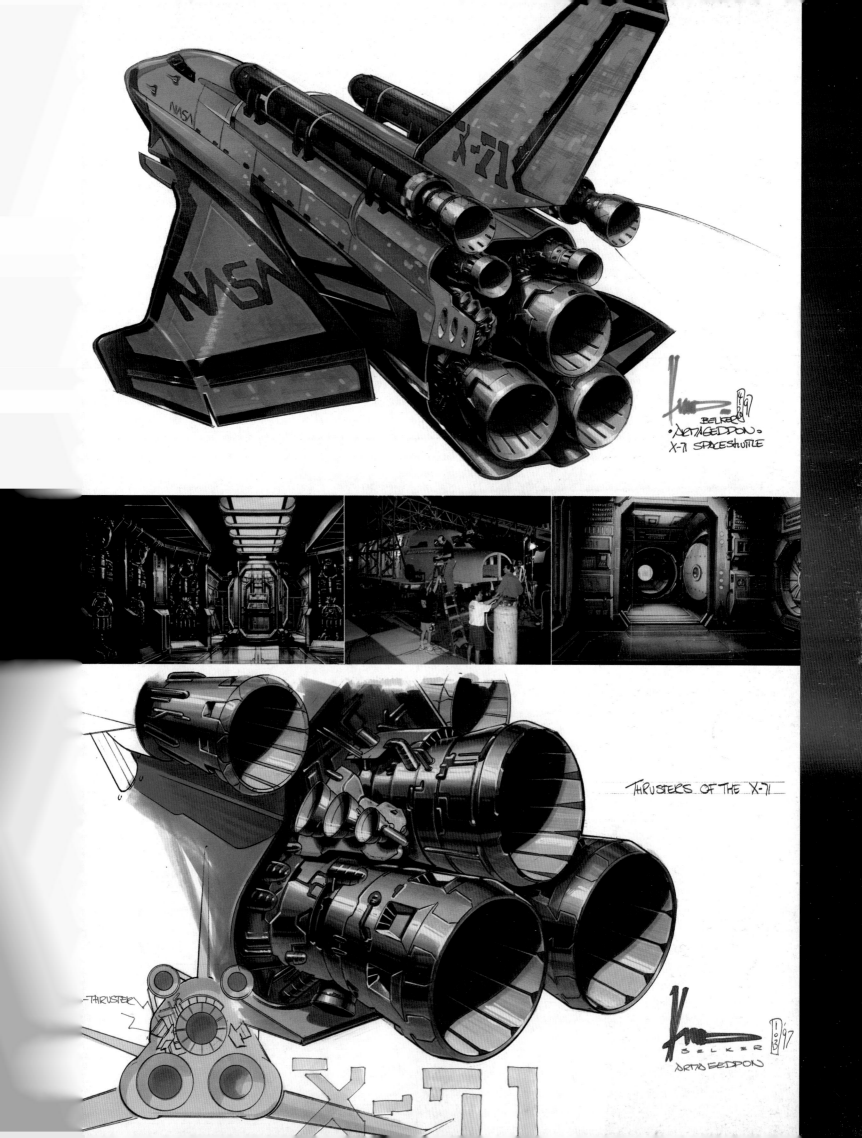

ARMAGEDDON
X-71 SPACE SHUTTLE

THRUSTERS OF THE X-71

THRUSTER

X-71

PRECEDING PAGES: Freedom crew. Left to right: Ken Campbell plays Max Lennert; Jessica Steen is NASA Copilot Watts; Will Patton plays Chick Chapple; Grayson McCouch is Lieutenant Gruber; Steve Buscemi is geologist Rockhound; Bruce Willis leads his team of drillers as Harry Stamper; William Fichtner is NASA's Colonel Sharp. Freedom crew patch design by Michael White and Illustrated by Edwin Natividad.

ABOVE: NASA team members, Copilot Tucker, Colonel Davis, Lieutenant Gruber, Copilot Watts, and Lieutenant Halsey, who accompany Harry and the rough-necks into space.

LEFT: The nuclear device being wheeled into the shuttle.

BELOW: The crawler transports the shuttle from the V. A. B. (Vehicle Assembly Building) to the gantry. This transport takes about four days.

FOLLOWING PAGES: A.J. and Grace say good-bye.

The hour of *Armageddon* is approaching. Harry and his roughnecks are ready for launch. Leading the mission is Colonel Sharp, played by William Fichtner (*Contact*, *Heat*), who is joined by five additional NASA personnel (two mission specialists and three other pilots). The mission personnel—astronauts and drillers—are divided into two seven-person teams.

On the launchpad two previously top-secret "X-71" Air Force shuttles are unveiled: *Freedom*, emblazoned in classic wartime-bomber style with a painted eagle icon, and *Independence*, its symbol a

"The X-71 model shuttle, like the look of the film, is very stylized," adds Richard Hoover, Dream Quest's visual effects supervisor. "They look more like fighter jets, sleeker and cooler-looking than real shuttles, with more wing, vents, thrusters, and the fighter-jockey emblems on the wings."

Like real shuttles, the X-71s would be pressurized—the technical term is "*encapsulated*"—so that helmets and suits could be removed in space. The major difference between a real shuttle and the final soundstage shuttle set built at Disney was the fictional shuttle's more spacious quarters, which made technical adviser Joe Allen a bit envious. "On one mission I flew with five [people], and you're really elbow-to-elbow, but you're well trained and once you get to orbit you can take the seats down, stow them away, and float around the cabin," Allen says. "That shuttle set is the Cadillac version."

The scene of the *Armageddon* shuttles' launch incorporates exclusive production footage of a real shuttle launch at the Kennedy Space Center. Pat McClung's visual effects team digitally composite an image of a 1/20-scale shuttle model onto the real rocket footage. (According to Allen, the thing that makes a shuttle launch look different from other launches is the airplane-configured ship itself—also called the "orbiter"—which is attached to an external tank and two solid rockets.)

Beyond shooting the launch at the full-scale, live-action "set," the filmmakers also had to create physical models and computer-generated versions of the shuttles. Deadline pressures forced the model departments of Vfx and Dream Quest each to craft its own X-71 spacecraft models. "There were concerns about matching with Vfx, but things went real well—you can't tell the different models apart," says Dream Quest visual effects art director Mike Stuart. "We used Vfx's molds and we just had to paint to match. Our shuttle was 1/20 scale—about seven feet long and made of epoxy and fiberglass with a six-point mount for the motion-control work. One of the big reasons we built our own shuttle was because our shot angles were a little different [from Vfx's] so we had to have different mounting points."

At the actual shuttle launch site the *Armageddon* crew, like all launch spectators, marveled at the blastoff's elemental force, an effect felt with earthshaking intensity even when viewed from outside the safety perimeter, miles away from the launchpad. "It was a real humid day, so we could literally see these shockwaves of energy rolling toward us," reports director of photography Schwartzman. "When a shuttle takes off at night the light is so bright it makes everything daylight for about ten seconds. Filming a launch live was the most exciting thing I've done in my life."

Although they filmed a daytime launch of the shuttle *Columbia*, the production team considered that a trial run for what they really wanted—to capture the spectacle of a night launch lighting up the sky. When the team arrived at Cape Canaveral in Florida in June 1997 for the night launch of the shuttle

Atlantis, they knew they'd have only one chance to get it right. "They only do night shuttle launches about every 18 months, so if we didn't get it we were screwed," Schwartzman recalls.

Weeks of planning between the production team and NASA anticipated every filming concern. Of the 15 cameras prepared to record the blastoff, 12 would be placed inside the three-mile safety perimeter (including one camera looking down from atop the launchpad itself). Because no one was allowed within the danger zone, a remote-control system had to be devised, with Schwartzman and NASA adapting the NASA computer responsible for launching the orbiter so that its signal would also turn the Panavision movie cameras on and off. (A separate countdown for the cameras opened the shutters seconds before ignition and closed them about a minute after the launch.) Schwartzman also had to calculate

film exposure levels for the pure burst of launch wattage that would, in less than two seconds, climb from 200 to 16,000 foot-candles of illumination. The cameras' lenses had to be fitted with special filters to protect them from the exhaust's wash of hydrochloric acid. To ensure that the cameras themselves wouldn't become flying projectiles, jettisoned by the launch's concussive blast, some 70 sandbags secured each instrument.

"The camera equipment withstood the launch, seemingly in perfect working order," Schwartzman recalls, "but I was very nervous until I got the report from the lab. But the stuff was beautiful. Every single camera provided a stunning piece of film."

The launch was but one of the challenges. Next, the production designers would have to create the look of shuttles flying through space and refueling at a *Mir*-like orbiting space station. And they would have to devise ways of showing *Freedom* and *Independence* making their slingshot arcs around the Moon, attaining the speed necessary for catching and landing on the oncoming asteroid.

PRECEDING PAGES: *A near quarter-scale model (almost 37-feet long) of the film's "X-71" super shuttle. The production's in-house Vfx visual effects unit prepared the model specifications and blueprints for Vision Crew Unlimited, which constructed the shuttle.*

RIGHT: *X-71 space shuttle launch bay. Art department illustration by Harald Belker.*

INSET: *Dream Quest Images computer-generated art of the space shuttle landing on the asteroid.*

LEFT: *Space shuttle launch. Art department illustration by Harald Belker.*

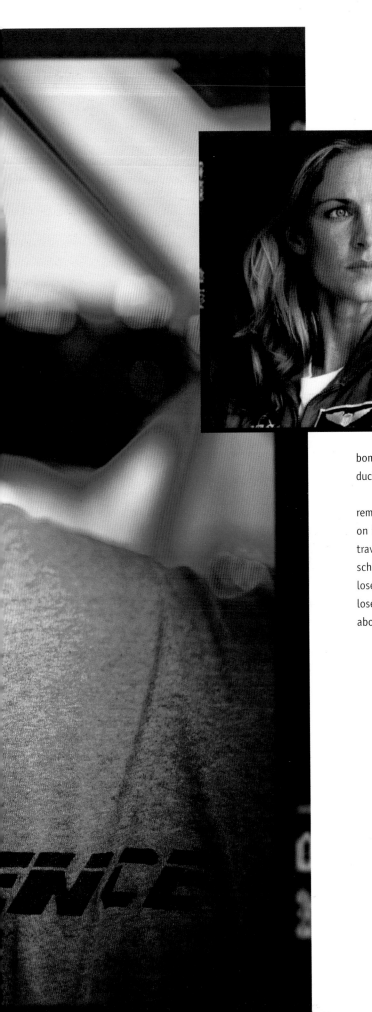

In the action scenes set on the rugged asteroid set, the actors themselves would go through all the trials and tribulations a blockbuster adventure movie can throw at a performer, from having to outrun pyrotechnic fire and bomb blasts as the space station explodes (in effect, accomplished on a full-scale set) to ducking flying boulders and debris on the asteroid—all the while keeping within character.

"I think a lot of people would have liked my character to be a little more gung-ho," remarks William Fichtner, who as Colonel Sharp flies with Harry, Chick, Rockhound, and company on the *Freedom* while A. J., a roughneck called Bear (Michael Clark Duncan), and the others travel aboard the *Independence*. "My character's an astronaut, probably out of the test pilot school at Edwards Air Force Base. Those guys are the real deal. The Right Stuff. They don't lose their cool, they don't get juiced up or pumped up a lot. I looked for every way not to lose my cool in this character—because they don't, no matter what's comin' down. It's all about completing the mission."

99

FAR LEFT: *Colonel Sharp [William Fichtner], overall leader of the mission to the asteroid. In the story, each shuttle—*Independence *and* Freedom*—carries four of Harry's roughnecks, two pilots, and a mission specialist.*

LEFT: *"Bear"—a member of the* Independence *team.*

ABOVE: *Copilot Watts [Jessica Steen].*

FOLLOWING PAGES:

TOP LEFT: *A rack of spacesuit costumes.*

BOTTOM LEFT: *Blue NASA mission launch suits.*

CENTER: *Harry and A.J. lead the roughneck team to action [Michael Clark Duncan in background].*

TOP RIGHT: *Space helmets.*

BOTTOM RIGHT: *Detail of roughneck spacesuit.*

PRECEDING PAGES: *Dream Quest Images makes the imagined real as the* Freedom *and* Independence *rocket into outer space in this final visual effects shot.*

RIGHT: *Ben Affleck experiences weightlessness, thanks to a wire rig, in the shuttle's cargo bay.*

LEFT AND INSET: *Billy Bob Thornton, as NASA's Dan Truman, reacts to Harry Stamper's video transmission from space.*

ABOVE: *NASA's Mission Control—Armageddon-style.*

OPPOSITE TOP: *Ben Affleck and Michael Bay.*

OPPOSITE BOTTOM: *Schwartzman makes a point with Will Patton and gaffer Andy Ryan.*

ABOVE: *Affleck and Bruckheimer on the asteroid set.*

FAR LEFT: *The Armadillo has its last tune-up and inspection in the O &C [Operations and Check-out Building].*

LEFT: *Miniature scale Armadillo built by craftsmen at Vfx.*

BELOW: *A production shot of the movie's X-71 shuttle on the Kennedy Space Center runway.*

TOP RIGHT: *Vfx model maker Dave Beasley puts the finishing touches on one of the shuttle scale models—the lightning bolt on the wing identifies this as the shuttle* Independence.

BOTTOM RIGHT: *Scale shuttle element being shot in front of greenscreen.*

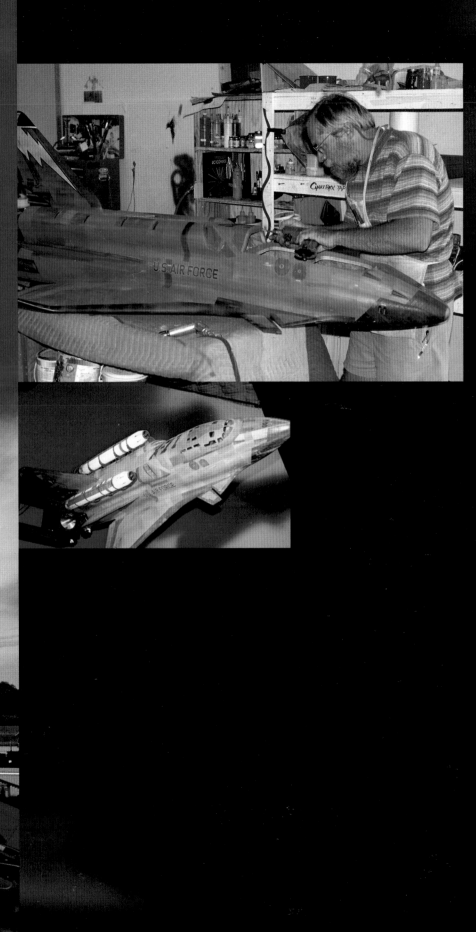

Karl [John Mahon] first discovers the incoming asteroid, and asks to name it after his wife, Dottie. Shot on location at Mount Wilson near Los Angeles.

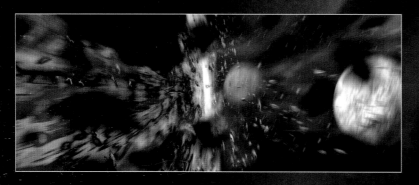

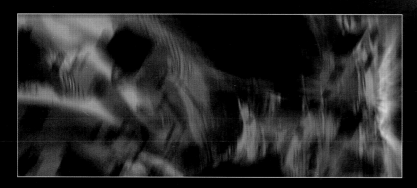

*Early Dream Quest Images concept art for the asteroid and its
gaseous vapors by Allen Battino.*

INSETS: *The Texas-sized killer hurtles past the Moon and
within striking distance of Earth in these Dream Quest Images
computer-generated concepts by Allen Battino.*

OPPOSITE TOP: *Interior views of the Russian Space Station.*

OPPOSITE BOTTOM: *Lev Andropov [Peter Stormare] looks out the space station porthole.*

LEFT: *The Russian Space Station. Note the bottom "T" that will accommodate the docking of the two shuttles. Art department concept illustration by Wil Rees. Model shop supervisor Alan Faucher's crew would make their scale model three times bigger than the real* Mir.

BELOW: *Despite Lev's diligent repairs to his home in space, the Russian Space Station succumbs to the elements and self-destructs.*

004 11 20:00
HRS MIN SEC MSEC

PART THREE

IN DEFENSE OF
EARTH

The asteroid set at Disney, when viewed from just within the soundstage doors, was surreal to behold. In the distance silhouettes of gigantic, spiky, stalagmitic rock formations rose from a stage that had been hollowed out and poured with concrete fashioned into rock-hard lava flows, sculpted rock shelves, and sheer cliffs. The shafts of light passing through openings in the sculpted rock formations made the terrain look organic, alien, and menacing. To simulate an asteroid's inhospitable environment, John Frazier's special effects crew triggered pyrotechnic explosions of asteroid shards, swung fake boulders on wires, even dropped huge columns of fake rock from the soundstage rafters.

While the bulk of the asteroid scenes (in which the oil drillers try to plant their nuclear device as the doomsday clock ticks down) were played out on the Disney set, the visual effects groups would conjure up the ships in space, from a refueling stop at the "Russian Space Station" to a ride past the Moon that catches the asteroid's fiery tail.

The scene in which *Freedom* and *Independence* stop at the Russian Space Station to refuel introduces lonesome Lev Andropov, Peter Stormare (*Fargo*, *The Big Lebowski*), a cosmonaut with a proprietary feeling about his creaky old home-away-from-home. The Russian Space Station, which ultimately explodes just as the shuttle crews manage to escape with Lev, is a wink at the actual Russian station *Mir*, which has been in Earth orbit since 1986. *Mir*'s well-publicized troubles have included a series of mini-disasters suffered in 1997—a breakdown in the oxygen system, an onboard fire, and a crisis set off when a remote-controlled cargo vessel smacked into a solar panel and broadsided one of the modules. Of course (and Lev could vouch for this), the aging *Mir* has also been a technological success, more than doubling its anticipated life span. The filmmakers identified the film's version generically as the Russian Space Station.

As with the shuttles, the space station was redesigned to serve the story while incorporating a contemporary realism. Here, too, the major artistic license was to create a bigger version

INSET LEFT: *Director of photography Schwartzman in the shadows of the asteroid set.*

ABOVE: *The rugged team of drillers faces the drama on the asteroid.*

of the real thing. According to Alan Faucher, Vfx's model-shop supervisor, the space station has the same basic design as Mir but is four times larger.

Two scale versions of the space station model were created by Vfx: a highly detailed 1/20-scale model crafted out of plexiglas and styrene and a pyrotechnic version built of cardboard and epoxy resins and constructed in two 1/12-scale sections. Of course, as Faucher notes, even a pyro model must be relatively detailed: "When you do a model explosion you can't have it exploding like an empty canister. You have to allow for what the camera will see."

While the space station was filmed on a motion-control stage at the Vfx unit's Culver City facility, the 1/12-scale pyro model was shot in the shop's parking lot and exploded in two separate sections, each hung from a cable 30 feet in the air and filmed with a high-speed motion-control camera. Adding to the pyrotechnic effect were the bags of blue liquid that Vfx special effects head Richard Stutsman packed inside the models. This liquid—a concoction of ethanol and a proprietary chemical—produced a blue flame that thrilled the director. In addition to maneuvering the camera, the motion-control technology also controlled the detonation of the miniature explosives.

"We shot the space-station pyrotechnics in two sections because it was too big to blow up all at once," explains project supervisor David Sanger. "There were so many different pyro cues

Camera operator Dave Emmerichs rides on a special camera chair [designed by Kenny Bates], hanging from the 70-foot ceiling of Stage 2.

Crash of the Independence as the shuttles enter the asteroid's atmosphere. Concept art by Dream Quest Images, artist Mike Meaker.

going off because it's supposed to look like a chain-reaction blast triggering multiple explosions within the whole length of the station. To do it all in one take would have required more timing boxes and detonators than we could load and program at one time. There once was a time, on a shot like this, when we could have loaded a couple cans of gasoline inside a model, put a fuse to it, and—Boom! But nowadays even the explosions have become more intricate. Even though it takes up a second of screen time there's all these multiple explosions crescendoing, all dressed to camera and with specific charges and detonators timed within a hundredth of a second to create a more sculptural blast."

Responsibility for creating the effects shots was split between Vfx, which handled the launch and the space station action, and Dream Quest, which took on the flight over the Moon. "Their shots were generally more high-speed," Dream Quest's Richard Hoover notes, "ours were more motion-control."

The so-called "Fly/Moon" sequence cut back and forth between Dream Quest's physical models of the *Freedom* and *Independence* shuttles and their computer-generated versions against a starfield, composited by Computer Film Company. "When the camera needed to be really close we used models, while shots of shuttles zooming long distances were more conducive to the CG versions because of the physical limits of shooting on stage," Hoover says.

Hoover adds that filmmakers have an advantage in creating the illusion of space travel—other than astronauts, earthlings haven't directly experienced the enormity of space. "When

Final visual effects for the explosion of the shuttle by Dream Quest Images.

you're creating outer space you're really dealing with the perception of space," he says. "We see space in film or in printed images, but it doesn't capture what you'd actually see with your own eyes. So we played with that."

The pass over the Moon used still images from NASA, altering them with a little digital magic. Employing a technique called texture mapping, Dream Quest could literally wrap the two-dimensional lunar photographs around a 3-D digital construct. Thus, a flat image could be rendered fully dimensional using light and shadow, with the free-flying "virtual" camera views of

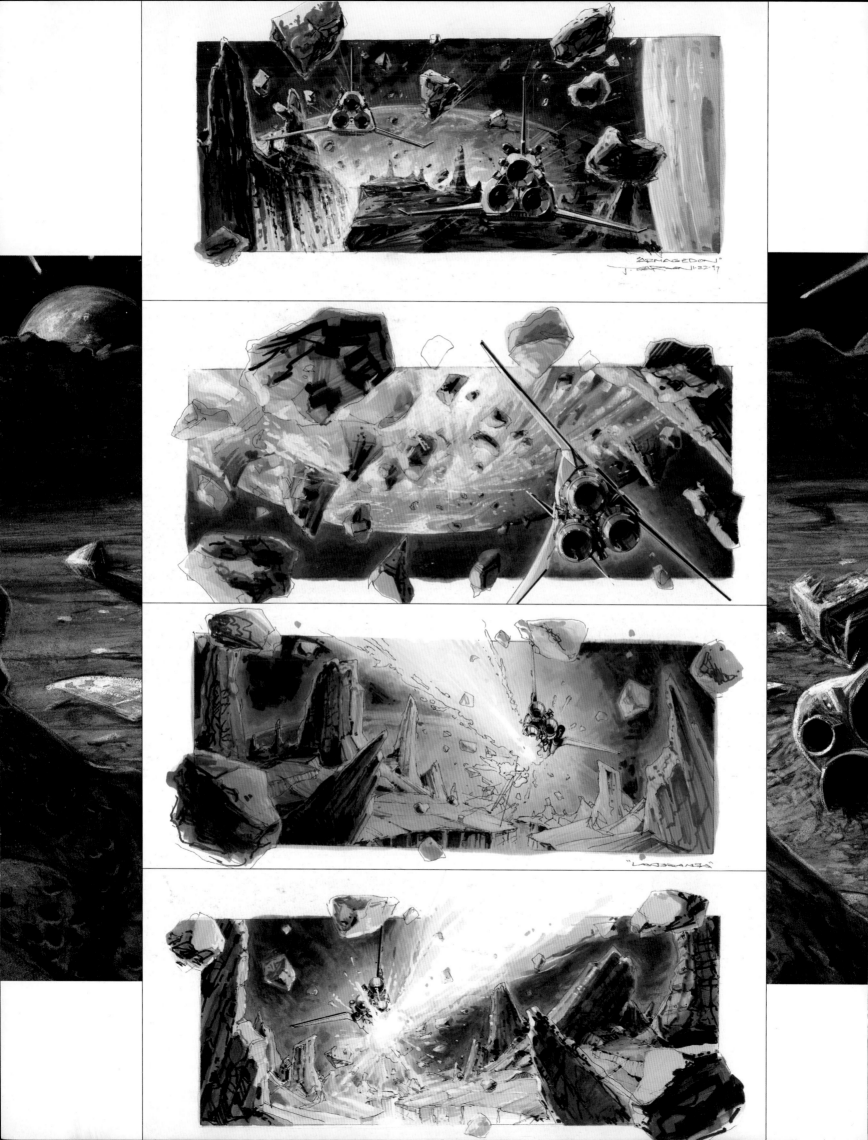

The production department worked out the look of the shuttle's asteroid approach, including the crash of the Independence and the rocky landing of the Freedom. [Illustration below by Tani Kunitake.] The live-action crash site scenes were staged in the Badlands of South Dakota.

"We bought dismantled parts of an L-1011 airplane in Arizona, painted them the shuttle colors, and trucked them to the location," says construction coordinator Greg Callas.

INSETS: Illustrations by Jim Carson.

"Michael Bay's visual style is very dynamic, so we had the shuttles flying close to the Moon's surface, giving a feel of speed and perspective," Hoover says. "We don't skim the surface, but we pass over the mountains and valleys, with added shuttle fire from the thrusters adding to the feeling of speed as they're hanging on for dear life."

Although the sequence in which the shuttles are slingshot around the Moon—their crews suffering crushing g-force—was deadly serious, creating the scene had its lighthearted moments. "We were supposed to be going 22,000 miles an hour, so I thought we'd be shooting in a wind tunnel or something—No!" laughs actress Jessica Steen (*Trial and Error*), who plays NASA Copilot Watts. "We had to act as if we had an elephant sitting on our chest. So, I'm making these horrific faces and Michael goes 'Cut! I'm trying to eat popcorn and you're grossing me out!' Oh, so you want a visually appealing elephant?! But Michael creates the reality. There's a specific dance he wants to see. He wants you to be on your toes and to give him what he wants."

Then, as the shuttles come into range of the killer asteroid, the storyline suddenly takes a shocking turn—the shuttle *Independence* smashes into the asteroid, killing most of its crew. The survivors, who include A. J. and Lev, are forced to use their undamaged Armadillo to search the asteroid for Harry and his team, who have successfully landed aboard the *Freedom*.

Bay likens *Armageddon*'s story structure to that of his film *The Rock*, which has long introductory scenes of a Navy SEALS team whose members, against audience expectations, meet sudden death during their assault on the renegade forces holding Alcatraz Island. "We spent enough screen time with the SEALS so you don't think anything bad is going to happen to them," Bay explains. "That's what we tried to do with *Armageddon*.

"The first hour we meet the characters, train them, have audiences fall in love with them. Then we launch them into space. We debated whether to take out the Russian Space Station scenes, but I

133

PRECEDING PAGES: *Liv Tyler as Grace Stamper.*

LEFT: *Ben Affleck as A.J. Frost.*

TOP RIGHT: *After makeup and costume, the last thing to go on is the helmet.*

BOTTOM RIGHT: *Ben Affleck gets suited up off set.*

PRECEDING PAGES: *"The special effects guys did a great job building the whole mechanized Armadillo vehicle,"* says construction coordinator Callas. *"My crew built the interior, what we call the 'buck'—it's on hydraulics and can rock up and down."*

ABOVE: *The Armadillo and spacesuited cast members at the scenes shot on location in the expansive South Dakota Badlands. The bulk of the stunts and drilling scenes would be played out on the Disney soundstage set.*

RIGHT: *A.J. and Bear take stock after surviving the crash of the* Independence.

felt the psychology was to put the characters in a life-or-death situation where the static about to blow up—and they get out alive! So the audience relaxes and thinks they're in action ride. We even slingshot the characters around the Moon and they go through g-for could kill a man, so now they've passed a second hurdle. But then we come up on the as and we lose one of the shuttles and some of our characters. Basically we changed the rul

As the shuttles approach the asteroid, they're battered by the debris—rocks, chunks ice—that's constantly cracking off the Texas-sized global killer. Now the shuttles are hea toward the asteroid's surface—one of them destined for a fatal impact, the other for safe down—and these scenes required the model-makers to contrive the asteroid's surface ter One of the models, built by Dream Quest and dubbed "the Tunnel," was a 60-foot-long ra scaled to look as if it were several miles across. From this otherworldly landscape, the fil to the effects work of *Independence*'s fiery crash and *Freedom*'s bumpy landing.

At its soundstage, Vfx executed the *Freedom* landing in two phases: First, a 1/12-sca (nearly eight-foot-long) shuttle model was flown from an overhead flying rig to simulate approach, with the model crashing through sculptured rock-formation set pieces. "I worke *Aliens* in England, and we dropped our model ships on wires—and we're still using the te nique," laughs supervisor McClung. "Model work isn't dead yet."

The set was then re-dressed with asteroid rock-formation pieces to represent the fin tance covered. For the last shot in the sequence, there's an effect of the model skidding stop along the set's 80-foot-long "crash stage."

"We had to work out of a standard warehouse that wasn't particularly movie-friendly did have some problems with the roof flexing as we flew the shuttle model—as it came l pulled the roof down about an inch," says Vfx special-effects supervisor Richard Stutsmar roof was 25 feet to the ceiling and we could have used another 20 feet easily.

"But for the landing itself Pat McClung wanted to see an old-fashioned skid, like bac high school days when you'd slam on the brakes and crank the wheel—'Starsky and Hutch is how he likened it," Stutsman grins. "When we filmed the approach we flew the model the opposite direction on the overhead track and had the model crash through a bunch o and rock formations which our illustrious model shop created to dress out the set."

Independence has crashed, *Freedom* has landed, and at this point in *Armageddon*'s st only hours before the asteroid will pass "zero barrier"—the threshold after which even a cessful drill and detonation of the atomic bomb won't be able to break up the asteroid ir to avoid a planetary collision. A. J. and Lev, with a mountain separating them from Harry the *Freedom* crew, use their Armadillo to reach their surviving mission comrades. Meanwh Harry stoically pushes forward; with the drill rigged on his Armadillo, he drills into the as oid—but the drill bit keeps breaking off. They're getting nowhere—and the vulnerable bl planet Earth appears over the horizon, "in the sights" of the global killer.

To heighten *Armageddon*'s dramatic tension, the asteroid itself would become a "cha ter"—the biggest, baddest evildoer in screen history. "After the shuttle flight action we r the villain—the asteroid," says Dream Quest's Hoover. "Up to then we've only seen hazy But then it comes into view. It's evil-looking."

As the asteroid moves into Earth's atmosphere, it begins to erupt and break apart, sending seismic shock waves, which throw Harry off-balance and scrambling for the detonator.

INSET LEFT: A crew member gets a fake boulder ready for action. Note the wires by which it hangs. Special effects would literally push these fake rocks over our heroes, simulating the upheavals on the alien terrain.

TOP RIGHT: Stairs lead seven feet below the asteroid set to the hydraulics system that John Frazier's crew built for a fake earthquake fissure.

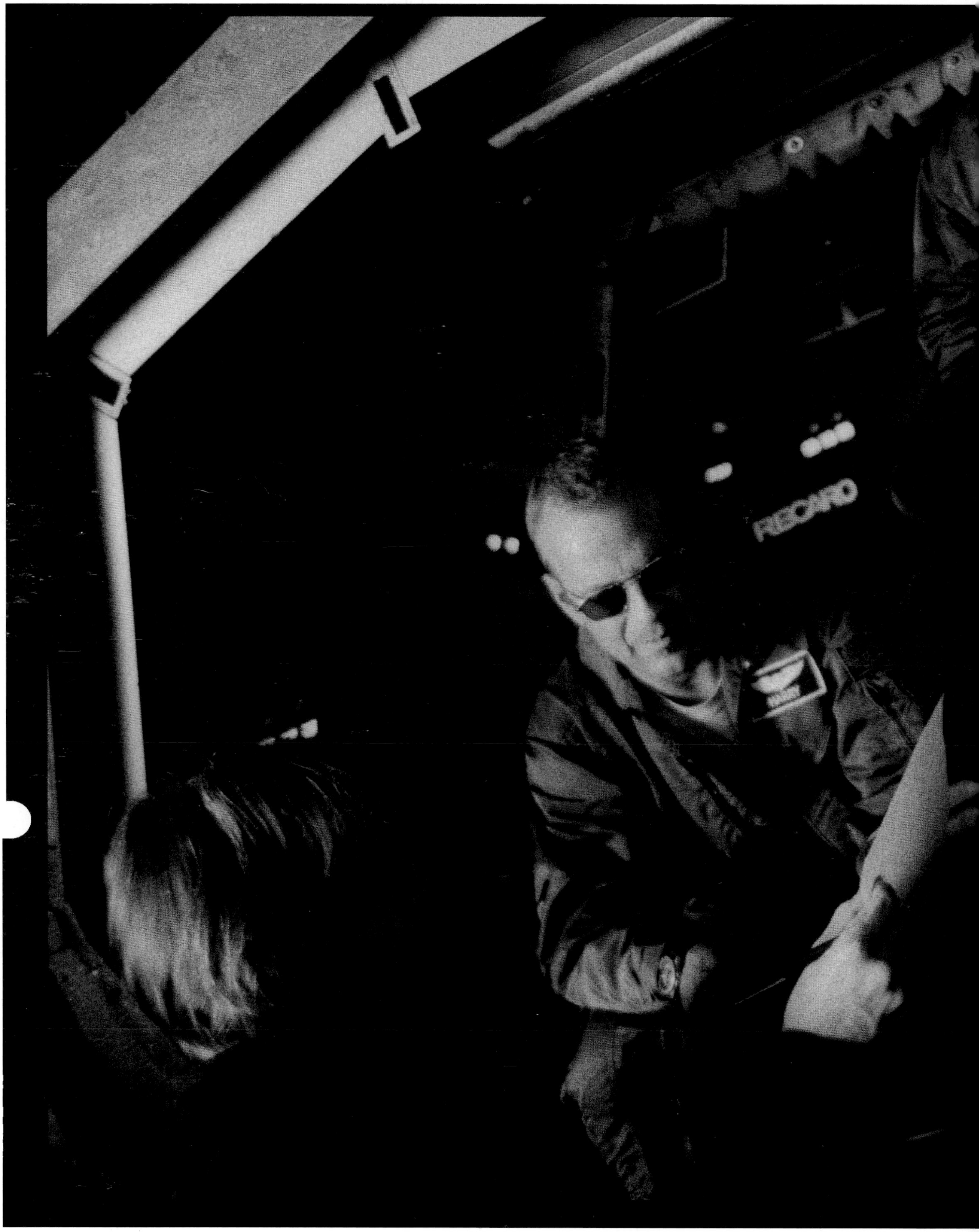
RECARO

PRECEDING PAGES: *A behind-the-scenes production still of the asteroid set on Stage 2 at Disney Studios.*

LEFT: *Bay directs Willis and Affleck in the shuttle* Freedom *set, a scale version that consultant Allen calls the Cadillac of shuttles.*

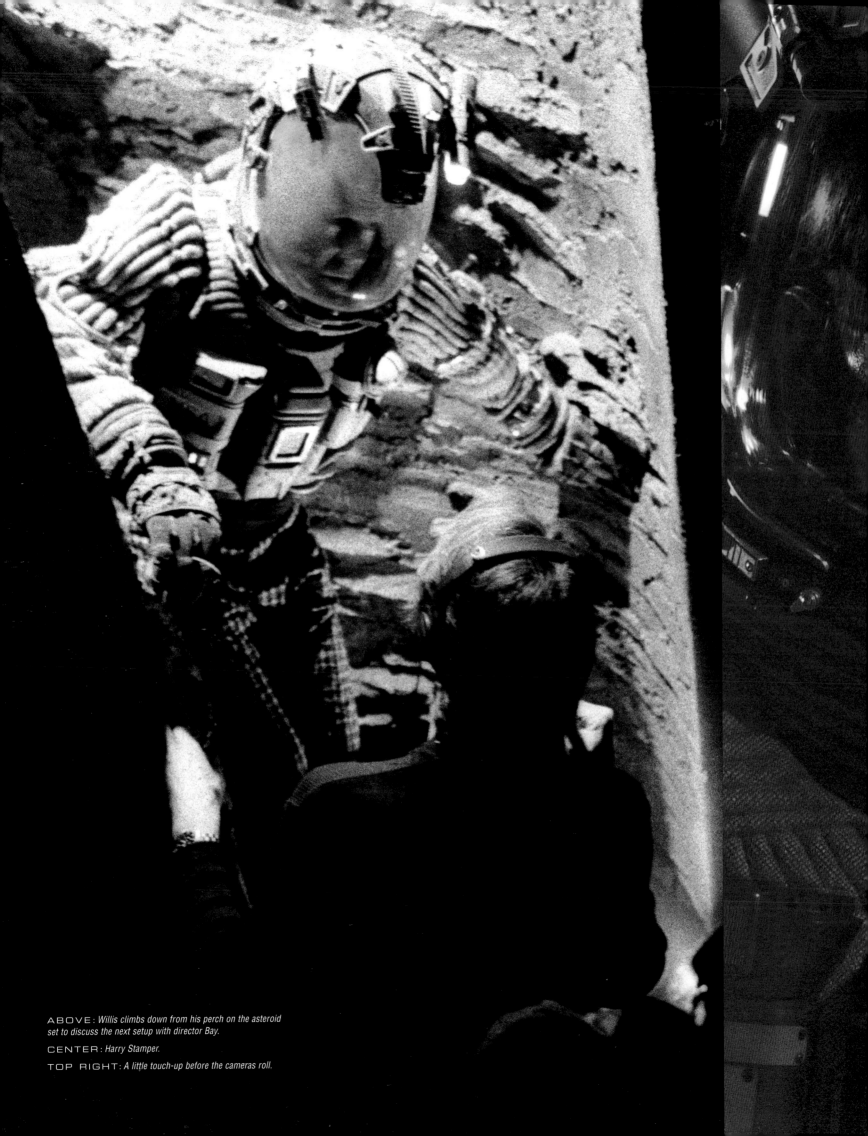

ABOVE: *Willis climbs down from his perch on the asteroid set to discuss the next setup with director Bay.*

CENTER: *Harry Stamper.*

TOP RIGHT: *A little touch-up before the cameras roll.*

It's the third week in January 1998, and down in the sculpted lava-flow of the asteroid set, at the very bottom of the open pit area, a helmeted and spacesuited Bruce Willis is slowly pulling himself up onto the side of the Armadillo. It is the actor's last day on the rugged set that has earned nicknames like "Hell Hole" and "The Pit of Despair" from the crew. Through his ComTex radio hookup with Willis, Michael Bay reminds his star that this will be his last shot on the asteroid set. . . .

"Of course his energy surged," Bay laughs. Willis scrambled to the top of the vehicle and the scene cut. The star turned to face the crew and, smiling through his helmet's face shield, bowed to their applause.

"We tried to make the asteroid as miserable as possible. This is a place you don't want to be," drawls John Frazier, whose team created everything from flying boulders to an ice storm.

The asteroid set was tough enough on the actors, but they also had to perform while moving around in hot, bulky, 70-pound spacesuits and helmets, topped off with heavy, functioning air packs strapped to their shoulders.

While the visual effects team could create its asteroid imagery using models and computer graphics, the physical set on which the actors would interact became reality only after the usual dance between art and commerce.

Originally, the *Armageddon* production team had hoped to construct the asteroid set in a blimp hangar in Orange County ("We got real big," construction coordinator Greg Callas recalls), but the studio arranged for the set to be built on the Burbank soundstage. A compromise was ultimately reached to achieve the scale Bay envisioned. Callas suggested a way to mimic the scale of a bigger facility: go underground.

"We certainly couldn't go up, so we took the stage floor out and went down about 30 feet," says Callas, whose recent work includes creating the Batcave for *Batman and Robin* and the Alcatraz sets of *The Rock*. "We brought in some engineers to look at the soil conditions and they drilled in the four corners of the stage. It's a raised foundation and there was between five and six feet of headroom underneath the floor joists. It was all sandy soil—it used to be a riverbed in the old days. The soil took compacting well, so then an outside construction company came in."

145

The perimeter of the soundstage was some 200 feet long by 140 feet wide, with the actual dig area about 90 by 70 feet, according to Callas's estimate. The stage, dug down to the old river bottom, was then built up with the infrastructure that would hold a slice of the landscape of the Texas-sized space rock—a particularly inhospitable territory full of giant, spiky rock formations. "Every eight feet there were 40-foot-long steel I-beams that were placed vertically and between those I-beams were placed what we call 'laggings,' four-by-twelves stacked up one upon the other," Callas details.

The asteroid set included a built-in roadway to accommodate the trucks and tractors needed for the engineering effort and—ultimately—to let the Armadillo be driven in for filming. "We had to be able to bring the Armadillo in and out of the set," Callas notes, "but the Armadillo weighed at least six times the weight of a single automobile. So we had to build a roadway that not only could withstand the Armadillo's weight but all the boom lifts—which themselves can weigh up to 50,000 pounds—and the equipment we needed to bring in to build the set."

The asteroid's topography was created out of concrete poured into the excavation. The rock spires were constructed with light steel frames and layered with foam sculpted into nightmarish shapes. The set's layout encompassed a variety of terrains, from the open pit area to rises thick with twisted stalagmitic rocks and ice-pick-sharp rock shards.

The newly dug stage-bottom was also fitted out with special hydraulic equipment to allow earthquake fissures to open up. "Our asteroid set floor goes down another seven feet, and that's where we put our hydraulics," Frazier explains. "Michael wanted the sense of this asteroid coming apart, but rather than doing a traditional movie earthquake, where you see the earth collapse, we came up with the idea of pulling the surface apart. There was a section about 30 feet square that the tractors dug out for us, and we built it as if it were a theme park ride. This section comes apart and then can come together for the next take. The operator underneath works the hydraulics and can also make steam come up through the fissure."

The compromises worked out between studio and production, though they did allow the imaginative extraterrestrial landscape to be built, presented challenges to director of photography Schwartzman, whose lighting and camera crew, which earlier had contended with NASA's land-of-the-giants scale, now had to deal with much tighter quarters.

"The set itself was large, but built wall-to-wall," Schwartzman says. "Every day was a challenge because we had to create this sense of light coming from the Sun, which is 93 million miles away, but in our stage the 'Sun' was only 55 feet away. The sharpness of light is determined by the distance of light to the subject, while the distance that I can move a light to a subject is defined by the space in which I'm filming. To increase that space we used every trick in the book, bouncing lights into mirrors and mylar, all of which helped effectively double the distance of the light and give it a sharper quality."

"We could take all the license we wanted on the asteroid because who's been on an asteroid? No one," adds designer Michael White. "Actually, our asteroid is nothing remotely like a real one, which is like a big chunk of undulating lava rock. Ours is the size of a small moon and has a harsh terrain and topography."

OPPOSITE: *Bay prepares Willis for a scene at the drill site.*

LEFT: *Special effects technicians dump a variety of breakfast cereals and Styrofoam to simulate asteroid debris.*

ABOVE: *The ground beneath the Armadillo begins splitting, causing its drill arm to jerk as the drill hole suddenly explodes. Rockhound [Steve Buscemi] is sent flying backward from the concussion.*

Stunts and effects on the asteroid set.

149

"The idea is that because there's so little gravity on this gigantic asteroid the rock formations are nothing like we're used to on Earth," adds Dream Quest senior vice president Keith Shartle, "so we have cantilevered rocks, spikes, strange formations. It's a fantastic, threatening environment."

According to Dream Quest art director Mike Stuart, director Bay did not want a ball-shaped asteroid, but a more dangerous looking body—something with a spiked tail, and with the tail itself trailing chunks of rock, ice, and other debris through space. The initial design of the rock and its terrain was worked out with small urethane-foam models Dream Quest created to show the director.

Bay liked these designs so much that he had Dream Quest create pieces to incorporate into the soundstage set, according to Stuart. "We built and painted spiky foreground rock formations that were movable and could be dressed to camera. We had a dozen really good sculptors here working on them. We had an advantage because early on we'd connected with the style of sculpting and painting they wanted while they were still underway with the massive undertaking of creating the Stage 2 set."

The designers built a two-foot-long asteroid model and scanned it to create a textured, three-dimensional mapped version. The main physical model of the asteroid—what effects people call the "hero" model—was some 25 feet long and looked, in Stuart's words, "like a turkey drumstick," with the giant spikes jutting from the end of the tail. "'Acid-dipped rock,' Michael [Bay] called it," Stuart continues.

"We shot our hero model motion-control on a greenscreen stage," Stuart explains. "The asteroid was built out of foam constructed over a steel armature, which we sculpted and detailed with bizarre shapes. The paint scheme varied from greens to blues to reds—even some glitter in there to simulate pockets of ice on the surface. Michael also wanted it to rotate in space, so we built an interior rotator mount at the heart of the armature which attached to the side of the asteroid that'd be away from camera."

Dream Quest created some eight different rock fragments, ranging in size from one foot to four feet in diameter, as motion-control elements to show chunks and shards of rock constantly breaking off the asteroid as it flew through space.

As a final touch, the designers created hellish vapors that would constantly issue from the fearsome asteroid's volatile surface. "We had people writing R&D software for six months to create the gases," says Richard Hoover. "One of the biggest parts of DQ's work in this film was making an asteroid look like something you've never seen before, so we have it spewing gases and erupting. The Hubble Telescope has taken a picture of a nebula that seemed effervescent and glowing, so we used that image as a guide to creating gases that glow and illuminate."

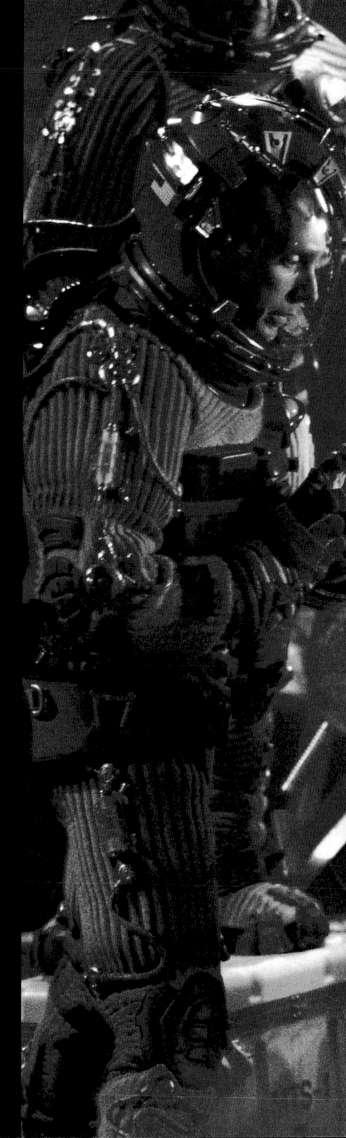

INSET ABOVE: *Harry and Colonel Sharp in a tense moment inside the shuttle Freedom.*

RIGHT: *Colonel Sharp, Chick Chapple, and Lieutenant Gruber get the drill going. While the prop drill-rig section worked on hydraulics to raise and lower the drill pipe, actual drilling shots were created using real drill bits in ground dressed to mimic the asteroid site. These would be seamlessly cut into the sequence. "Movie magic!" John Frazier exults.*

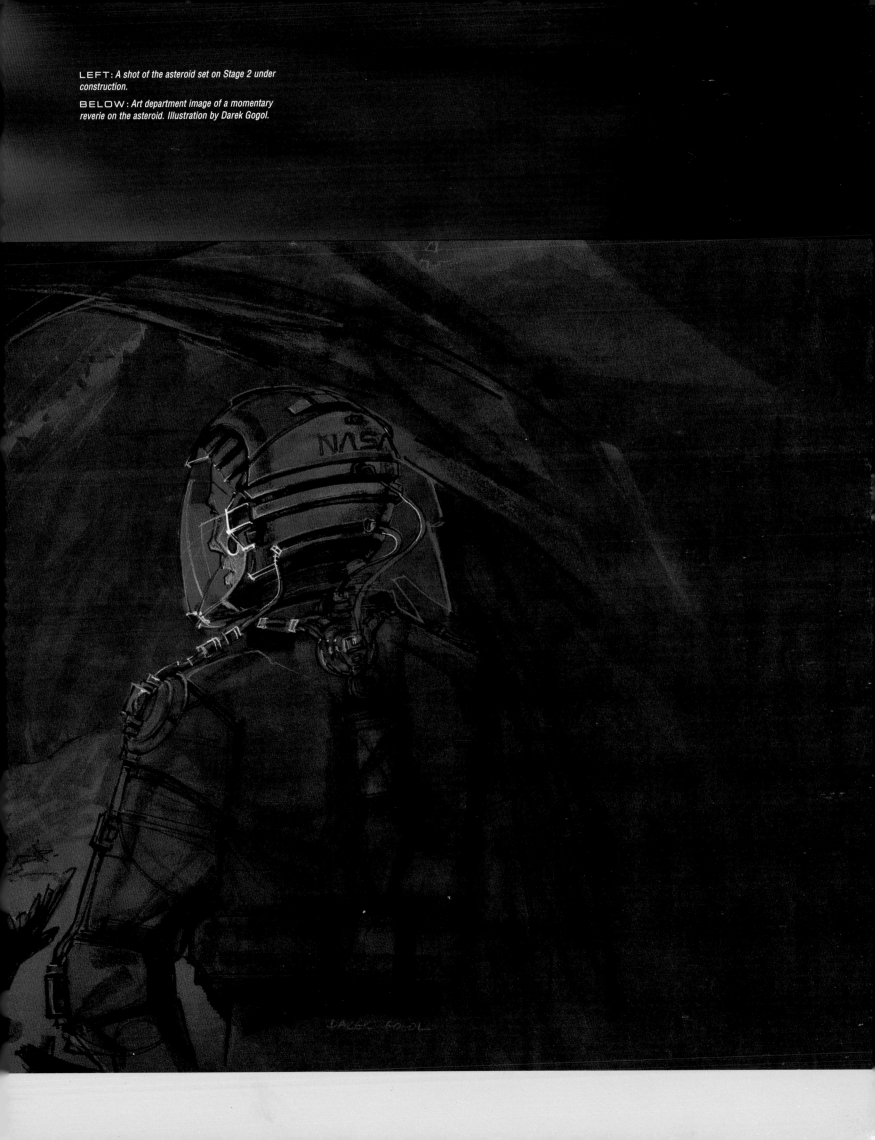

LEFT: *A shot of the asteroid set on Stage 2 under construction.*

BELOW: *Art department image of a momentary reverie on the asteroid. Illustration by Darek Gogol.*

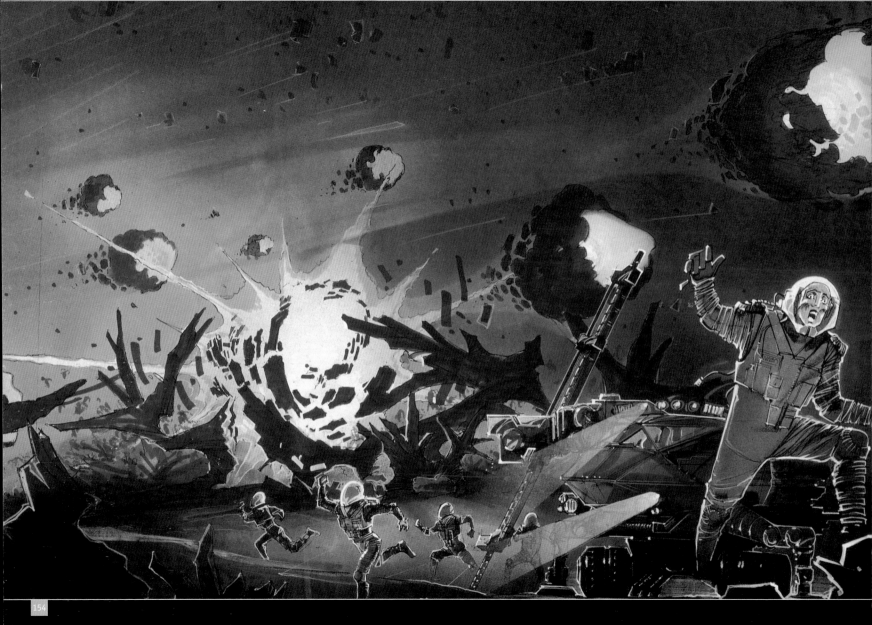

155

OPPOSITE: *All hell breaks loose in this art depart-ment conception. Illustration by Darek Gogol.*

ABOVE: *Safety shields are a must for those close to the action, especially when pyrotechnics and fan-blown particles begin to fly. Special effects technician Joe Pancake gives a boulder an extra added push for good measure.*

Although Hollywood dramatics necessitated an imminent cosmic disaster (including the white-knuckle standard of a clock ticking down), the premise of sending a team into space to destroy or deflect the asteroid is theoretically possible, particularly if an early warning system were in place that would give humankind years, not just a few weeks, in which to prepare and respond.

Even given the Armageddon mission's theoretical possibility, however, the script does take a few liberties: for instance, a single nuclear bomb probably couldn't break apart a Texas-sized asteroid. ("Well, it's a really big bomb," one production member offered helpfully.)

Consultant Ivan Bekey hypothesizes that "if you had five years available you could send a robotics ship or a manned ship to drill a hole in an asteroid, insert a couple of nuclear bombs, and detonate them by remote control, which would be adequate to change the asteroid's orbit enough to miss Earth. In a realistic situation time is of the essence. But there are studies that show it can be done, and I have run the trajectories myself. If manned, it would have to be an interplanetary spaceship much larger than the shuttle and it would have to be in space for a number of years.

"By the way," Bekey continues, "the Air Force is interested in planetary defense, in missions to protect the Earth. They see it as an extension of their job to protect the nation from incoming ballistic missiles."

But Bekey observes that the money hasn't really been forthcoming for efforts to keep watching the skies. "The asteroid that missed us a couple years ago was another dinosaur-extinction rock—and we didn't know about it until it'd passed! It would have been the biggest disaster mankind has faced. You would have had no warning—and all of a sudden it would be nuclear winter."

At this moment in time, if an asteroid would suddenly be sighted in range of Earth, humankind would have one recourse, according to Bekey: "Pray."

Early in the production, some Armadillo asteroid action was shot in front of a greenscreen onstage in Burbank.

INSETS: *All hell breaks loose on the set.*

What's the true measure of a hero? It's the million-dollar question the drillers and astronauts must ask themselves in *Armageddon*.

The bomb is ready for detonation, and the zero barrier is fast approaching, but because of a mishap the nuclear device can't be exploded by remote control—it has to be detonated manually. The surviving roughnecks and NASA astronauts draw straws.

As the production drew to a close, the cast and crew began to recognize the enormity of the project they'd been involved in. Many were grateful for the chance to jump into a no-holds-barred Jerry Bruckheimer production, while others marveled at the stunning visuals that Bay was producing. During the final days, many of the performers—after weeks of trudging onto the asteroid set, day after day, encumbered by their heavy spacesuits—would comment on how incredible it was all looking on film. "I watched the trailer and I sat there frozen—I got goose bumps, because it was so strange to me," Liv Tyler smiles. "My first few weeks had been two-second reactions to things that weren't happening, and I'd never done acting like that before. But it was so amazing to see the finished product, how all the different pieces fit together."

The end of a production is a bittersweet time. The caravan, which has gathered together a community dedicated to conjuring up thrills for the planet's moviegoers, finally pulls down its tents, and everyone scatters to the four winds. "Making a movie is like forming a corporation," says Vfx's Richard Stutsman. "You get hundreds of people together, you steamroll it through, and then you dissolve the corporation. It amazes me when you see the last guy sweeping the floors of a set and you close the doors and it's an empty warehouse that just months earlier had all this activity. A movie production is something that grows, then it disappears and becomes a distant memory."

Beyond its blockbuster budget and star power, *Armageddon* had basked in the reflected glory of "the real thing." Everyone who'd worked on the film—from Bruckheimer and Bay to actors and crew—repeated like a mantra that the great joy of moviemaking is the passage it affords into other places and other lives—things you might otherwise never get to experience. And over the months of its making, Armageddon had brought a host of real-life heroes—oil drillers, flyboys, even space travelers—into its orbit.

LEFT: *Harry struggles to reach the detonation box.*

CENTER: *Concept art of front of asteroid as nuclear detonation splits it in half. Dream Quest Images concept art by Mike Meaker.*

RIGHT: *On location in South Dakota.*

ABOVE: *A.J. protests after Harry has
pushed him back into the shuttle.*

RIGHT: *Harry Stamper grips the nuclear
detonator—and his American flag.*

INSETS [ALL]:

Return of the astronauts played out on the NASA space shuttle runway.

CENTER: *The NASA team, headed by Dan Truman (Billy Bob Thornton) and Walter Clark (Chris Ellis) celebrates Earth's victory.*

For executive producer Jim Van Wyck, who had spearheaded so much of the production's logistics, a favorite memory was the extra flourish that lights up the film's finale. The scene required a two-day shoot at the Kennedy Space Center.

On the first day of the shoot, Van Wyck heard that the Air Force Thunderbird precision flying team would be performing at a nearby air show. A bolt of inspiration got him on the phone to Chuck Davis, the film's Air Force liaison.

"Chuck had been with us but was on his way back to L.A., so I basically left a message at his home," Van Wyck recalls. "I asked him if there was any way the Thunderbirds could do a flyover we could photograph, to be part of this whole thing?

"Chuck called me back at midnight that night. He loved the idea because a Thunderbird flyover is the best salute in the world. At four o'clock that morning Chuck called Nellis Air Force base [located outside Las Vegas], the home of the Thunderbirds, as well as the head of public relations for the Air Force and Pentagon. By two o'clock in the afternoon the next day he had confirmation the Thunderbirds would fly over our set on the shuttle landing facility. We were on radio to the tower, which was on the radio with the Thunderbirds, and at 3:30 we got the word they were heading our way. Five jets came out of the sky, did a low pass over our set, and popped the smoke as they flew overhead. I got goose bumps watching the Thunderbirds. That was all Chuck Davis. For me that epitomizes the level of cooperation we got from the Air Force and NASA on this picture."

Some of the actors, like Will Patton, gloried in the marathon run of the action blockbuster. Patton wore the nicks he'd caught on the side of his face like badges of honor. He didn't even remember how he'd gotten them: probably a lick of fire from the full-scale space station explosion. "You're bound to get a little scratch here and there," he grins, "with all the running and fire and explosions. At times this movie felt like being in some kind of military training! The asteroid set was pretty extreme. It's like we got that feeling that you're in the middle of outer space trying to save the world—and it's impossible! You have to fight fires, explosions, rock storms. Every day it really felt like I was going through it for real. The timing was real important because a few feet one way or the other was some pretty serious stuff—which was sort of fun! I got to the point where I asked Michael to put me in the middle of the dangerous action as much as possible.

"Actually, I used to enjoy doing theater because there were so many things you could do with your body," Patton adds. "But as I got into film it became more confining. But with so much physical stuff in this movie, I got to use my body the same way I did on stage. The thing about an action movie is you wait for the cameras to roll and then, suddenly, there's a 30-second burst of intensity where your best friend is dying or there's some cataclysmic event. For the first time in my life I've started thinking that maybe action movies are where it's at!"

William Fichtner echoes Patton's sentiment: "I've been on the asteroid, I've been on the space station when it was spinning in circles and it was blowing up and they were throwing tree sap on the back of my head because the flames were going right by me—this thing got wild!

PRECEDING PAGES: *The production chose a hallowed spot at Kennedy Space Center, site of the Apollo 1* tragedy, *to play a poignant scene between Harry and his daughter, Grace.*

TOP: *Bruce Willis, Jerry Bruckheimer, and Michael Bay.*

ABOVE: *Director Bay's NASA jacket.*

"One of the reasons I was interested in working on *Armageddon* was because I wanted to spend time around the guys who did this, the fighter and test pilots. During the production I met the guy who was head of the test pilot school at Edwards Air Force Base. Just about everybody in the test pilot school wants to get to NASA to pilot the shuttles. He told me you might be a test pilot with nerves of steel and still not get to NASA because the space agency is looking for more than just the best pilots—it's looking at demeanor, personality, the whole package. He impressed me because here's a guy who's a god when he walks down that hallway—he is the Man—and he told me: 'I'm applying to get to NASA.' And he gave me a thumbs-up. You watch this guy and you think it can't get higher than this. But to him—yeah. There was another thing. There was space."

For the whole production, one of the most exciting sidelights had been the opportunity to go behind the scenes at NASA. Tyler talks about the night they stopped shooting to watch a satellite launched—a real rush for someone too young to have seen men walk on the Moon live. (Liv's earliest memory of space travel is the *Challenger* disaster.) "At night when the rocket goes up the whole sky lights up," she recalls, "and the noise hits you all of a sudden. It's beautiful."

Then there were more poignant moments—notably a pre-launch scene between Willis and Tyler shot at the site of the *Apollo 1* disaster. It was a haunting stage on which to play a scene about regret and forgiveness. To the men and women of the space program this is sacred ground, a place where astronauts have come to meditate on the valor of their predecessors, to pray, to contemplate history. The site's been left to decay with time, and the Florida jungle is reclaiming it. "We were instructed that the site is very sacred," Greg Callas says. "The launch site is totally removed from the other facilities and is left to itself. It was strange to see. It's deteriorating and almost looks like Stonehenge, with these big concrete columns and a round steel ring that's all rusted with vines growing on it."

NASA consultant Joe Allen's recollections may seem a bit incongruous, given *Armageddon*'s premise of a global-killer asteroid, but for him the project brought back memories of floating in space, seeing the home planet whole. "In space there's no atmosphere, so everything's glorious and infinitely clear. You feel such serenity," says Allen. "When I was tethered during one of my spacewalks, there was time to look at the Earth. Two-thirds of the time you spend over gorgeous ocean and cloud, a third over the continents. I was spacewalking for eight hours, and during that period you go around Earth five times. You'll see sunrises so brilliant you can't look at them—you have heavy face shields you put down to protect you. Then the Earth turns, blocking the Sun, and you're in total darkness for about 45 minutes, except for your space shuttle, which is brilliantly lit like a ballpark at night.

"I read this great quote from a space flyer who said something that's so true. Basically, when you're out in space the first day in orbit you try to find your home. Then the next day you become quite interested in the various continents. And by the third day all the crew members are just looking at the beauty of the Earth."

As *Armageddon* was wrapping first-unit work, the unmanned Near Earth Asteroid Rendezvous (NEAR), which had been launched in February 1996 and had already completed a flyby of the asteroid Mathilde, made a return pass some 330 miles above the Earth. Using a gravity-powered slingshot effect, NEAR pulled away from the planet at an estimated 15,000 miles per hour, heading off on its year-long journey toward a rendezvous with its mission target: asteroid 433 Eros, a 30-mile-long rock orbiting the Sun between Earth and Mars.

As Gale Anne Hurd said: "There's always a basis in reality for an idea."

"I think *Armageddon* will raise public awareness of asteroids," producer Bruckheimer reflects. "Certainly the media will pick up on it and discover for themselves, as we did with our own research, the probability that we'll be hit by an asteroid sometime in the future.

"The scope of this picture was of epic proportions. It was amazing the cooperation and access we got from NASA and the Air Force. It was exciting to see a B-2 bomber and a shuttle launch live—those are things you'll remember for the rest of your life. On a movie like this you're always burning up brain cells at the beginning and at the end. It was a long haul, with over 100 days of filming, but we brought it in on budget. It was creatively rewarding to climb the mountain again."

LEFT: *Will Patton, Steve Buscemi, Bruce Willis, Liv Tyler, Ben Affleck, Ken Campbell, and Michael Duncan pose for the camera.*

FOLLOWING PAGES: *At left, Harry Stamper, All-American Hero. At right, the Thunderbirds pay tribute as Grace and A.J. look to the heavens.*

Armageddon *cast and crew assemble on the Mission Control set.*

ACKNOWLEDGMENTS

Special thanks to Michael Eisner, Joe Roth, and Dick Cook for giving us the green light on this massive undertaking and to those listed to the right who worked tirelessly to make this book possible. And to everyone at the Walt Disney Studios, Jerry Bruckheimer Films, Bay Films, NASA, Johnson Space Center, Kennedy Space Center, and the United States Department of Defense who supported our efforts throughout the production, our heartfelt gratitude.

JERRY BRUCKHEIMER

Daniel Albelo
Teri Avanian
Oren Aviv
Tony Barbera
Tracy Bennett
Stacey Byers
Jenny Campbell
Deborah Caple
Michael Cooper
John Cywinski
Donald DeLine
Ann-Marie DeWinkeleer
Rae Griffith-Gagnon
GP Color/Emerald City
Richard Hoover
Lisa Kitei
Jennifer Klein
Michael Mendenhall
Pat McClung

Sylvain Michaelis
Bob Miller
Chad Oman
John Pisani
Raul Ramirez
Mary Reardon
KristieAnne Reed
Diane Sabatini
John Sabel
Pat Sandston
Brad Sisk
Mike Stenson
Philipp Timme
Barry Waldman
West Coast Photo
Jim Van Wyck
Kristin White
Michael White
Pam Wilkins

NASA HEADQUARTERS

Bobbie Faye Ferguson
Dan Golden
Bertram Ulrich
Peggy Wilhide

KENNEDY SPACE CENTER

Roy Bridges
John Graves
Tina Greer
Hugh Harris
Bill Johnson
Lisa Malone
Margaret Persinger
Dan Thompson

JOHNSON SPACE CENTER

George Abbey
Ron Farris
Douglas Ward
Jean Womack

U.S. DEPARTMENT OF DEFENSE

Charles E. Davis
John P. Haire
Gary L. Hatch
Colonel John Martin
Ron Sconyers
Phil Strub
Ken Warren
Lt. Colonel Robert C. Williams